The original flag of the former South Vietnam, known as the Vietnamese Heritage and Freedom flag.

Stranger in Saigon

With the
British Medical Team
in South Vietnam
1968-1971

For Anthony Hall
from Martin Slater.

Stranger in Saigon

Martin Slater

With the
British Medical Team
in South Vietnam
1968-1971

MILLERSFORD PRESS

Stranger in Saigon

With the British Medical Team in South Vietnam 1968-1971.
© Martin Slater 2022

Front cover image: The traffic and pollution in Saigon. © Martin Slater

Frontispiece: Vietnamese on the top road in Kontum. © Martin Slater

ISBN 978-0-9572736-8-9
A CIP record of this book is available from the British Library.

Edited and designed by Sonia Aarons-Green.
First published in the United Kingdom in 2022
by Millersford Press, Woodgreen Road,
Godshill, Hampshire, SP6 2LP.
www.millersford.co.uk
Printed by Biddles Books Ltd.

All images and text © Martin Slater

For the members of the British Medical Team
who shared my experience in Vietnam,
and medical laboratory colleagues everywhere.

CONTENTS

ACKNOWLEDGEMENTS

I am indebted to my friends Fenella and the late David Wood for their kind permission to include their email in my text. This e-mail corrects some of my misunderstandings.

Thanks to my sister, Mrs Eithne Thornton, who first typed notes from my rambling dictation on cassette tapes about my time in Vietnam. Notes which gave me the courage to start typing on my own.

Thanks to my niece, Dr Catriona Bonfiglioli, who made many helpful comments on an early draft in 2002 and later versions, and my friend Mr Roderick Standing who proofread the second draft. Thanks to Mrs Jill Bentley for her recent encouraging remarks and the late Dr Joan Guy for her generous discouragement.

Especial thanks to Mr Robin West who has given much time and the use of his invaluable computer skills to help me prepare an illustrated version of this essay. In the end there are more photos than text. Thank you, Robin. Without you many photos would still be fading and forgotten in my loft. The written text, with its many deficiencies, remains entirely my responsibility.

Finally, thanks to my editor, Sonia Aarons-Green, for transforming a rather odd document into book form.

Martin Slater
Southampton
January 2022

PEOPLE MENTIONED IN THE TEXT

Mrs Peta Andrea Team Radiographer and a great friend of mine. Later Mrs Walters.

Brian Staley Reporter and friend of Dr Adrian Pointer.

Gordon Barclay Surgeon, Quaker and philanthropist.

Dr John Bass South African doctor who worked in the refugee camps.

Bill Collis Doctor in the team who left fairly soon after I arrived.

Dr John Clarke Mentor to me. Took over surgery after the first surgeon was repatriated.

Cô Tinh Very bright technician who swam. Later escaped to California.

Gerry Chavasse Embassy information officer and Vietnamese specialist.

Barbara Corvino American nurse at Minh Qui hospital in Kontum.

Shirley Crosman First cousin in Mason City, USA.

Peter J Curtis Married to Chantal, my mother's lodger. Australian Ambassador, Laos.

Dan Ong Dan the lavatory man. Nhi-Đồng plumber and Chi Hai's boyfriend.

Dược Sĩ Anh Doctor/Pharmacist director of Bệnh-Viện Nhi-Đồng laboratory.

Geoff Bulley Engineer at Minh Qui and later administrator for LEPRA in Malawi.

Douglas Gray Nurse and Catholic pacifist, in Vietnam under his own steam.

Dr Joan Guy Pathologist in Southampton and Boss at Nhi-Đồng Oct - Dec 1968.

Dr Tom Hughes Davies Paediatrician Team leader from 1969 to early 1971.

Mike Inman Anaesthetist at the start of the Team. He obtained our PX privileges.

Jenny Jones Nurse who survived a horrific road accident.

Mr Luan Vietnamese nurse/anaesthetist who became our administrator.

Barry Mallett MLSO colleague and friend in Southampton.

Mr Mau Vietnamese colleague at Nhi-Đồng laboratory.

Monsieur Pierre Embassy factotum and Mr Fixit.

Monsieur Tam Older French speaking colleague at Nhi-Đồng laboratory.

Mike Coles Ex-army American paramedic who worked at Minh Qui hospital.

Dr Duncan McCauley Team leader in post when I arrived in October 1968.

Dr Bác Sĩ Hoang Khai Nguyen Vietnamese pathologist at Nhi-Đồng.

Nglau Ong Montagnard laboratory technician at Minh Qui hospital.

Pam Fisher Nurse who married Tom Wynn from the Embassy.

Jean Platz Dr Pat Smith's right hand woman at Minh Qui hospital.

Dr David Poole Doctor in the Team and the last to go.

Ray Berry Southampton biochemist.

Dr Douglas Stanley My pathologist boss in Vietnam, late 1969.

Dr Pat Smith Minh Qui doctor and legendary for work with the Montagnards.

Tom Carlton Anorexic ex-army helper at Minh Qui.

Ya Calixt Montagnard nun/nurse/laboratory technician.

TITLES AND TERMS OF ADDRESS

English, French, Vietnamese and Bahnar (a Montagnard language) terms of address are used interchangeably in the text. I tended to use the titles that I heard other people using. Thus, Monsieur Pierre was always Monsieur Pierre while Mr Luan was mostly Mr Luan but sometimes Ong Luan...

VIETNAMESE

Ông pronounced om = Sir
Ông Mỹ = Mr American *
Cô = Miss
Bà = Madam or Mrs
Chi = Elder sister
Chi Hai (Sister two) = Senior woman servant
Bác = Uncle
Bác Sĩ = Doctor
Dược Sĩ = Pharmacist
*Used by urchins and accompanied with the 'Round Eye' gesture.

BAHNAR

Ya = Grandmother: a term of respect
Ya Pơgang = Woman doctor
Bok = Sir

INTRODUCTION

Central to this book is the pathology laboratory of the Saigon Children's hospital. In Vietnamese: *Phòng Thí-Nghiệm, Bệnh-Viện Nhi-Đồng.* Literally translated something like: Room-Test, Sick Institute Little-Children. We always referred to the Hospital as *Nhi-Đồng* - Little Children - and I will do so in this text.

I was somewhat naïve and untravelled when I arrived in Vietnam; I found the places and people fascinating. The laboratory was rather strange but not wholly unfamiliar which is why I have written less about it and more about places and people. None the less, the laboratory is pivotal to my account of my time in Vietnam. I was a Medical Laboratory Scientific Officer (MLSO) and working in the lab was the reason I went there and was granted a visa.

I wrote these reminiscences years later, long after I had retired. The photographs were taken then and there. I used to develop my black and white negatives in Saigon and only printed them when I finally returned to England. In those days, we bought colour slides with the cost of postage and development included in the price. Kodak did mine and sent them to my home in England. The decades had long degraded the transparencies, and my friend Robin West has done much splendid work in restoring them to something like their original state and colour, in some cases better.

A few very brief notes are required, since all of this happened so far away and long ago. Vietnam ceased to be a French colony after the battle of Dien Benh Phu in 1954. By 1968, the country was divided into a communist North and a republican South by the demilitarised zone (DMZ), on the 17th parallel of latitude. The communist North, supported by Russia and China, was fighting to reunite North and South while South Vietnam was trying to remain independent with the help of the 'Free World Nations'. The help

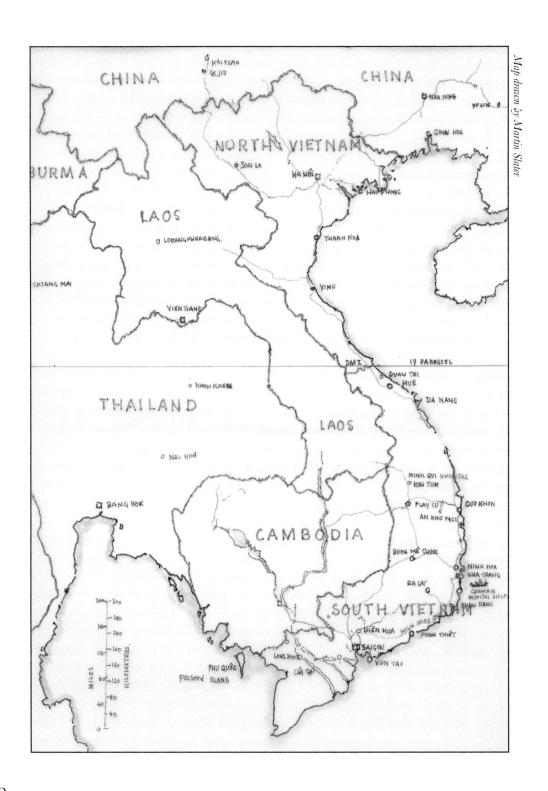

was mainly military, and mainly American. President Johnson of the United States urged Prime Minister Wilson to contribute to the war. Wilson declined to send in our soldiers but instead sent us: the British Medical Team.

The British Medical Team, under various Team leaders and personnel, ran in Saigon from 1966 till early 1971. Part of the time the team had a pathologist, and one of the pathologists thought that a British laboratory technician might be a good idea; hence my presence there.

Áo dài, the colourful and elegant traditional dress of Vietnamese women.

CHAPTER 1

THE REASONS WHY

You have my cousin Nicholas Slater to thank for these recollections. Nicholas said that he was writing a book on blood. I told him that blood had been part of my job as a Medical Laboratory Scientific Officer and I could contribute one or two items to his book. I started to jot down a few anecdotes and this encouraged me to write more on the time I spent with the British Medical Team in Vietnam, from October 1968 until early in 1971.

Among other things, I hoped to provoke other people from the Team to record their own, potentially more exciting, impressions. I also hoped it would satisfy the elderly family archivist, John Slater. One of the Team said to me that, after thirty years, her memories of those times have taken on a dream-like quality. I feel rather the same.

I should explain what an 'Em-less-oh' is. I started my working life as what was, in effect, an apprentice Medical Laboratory Technician. When I qualified I was told: "Technicians are rather inferior people who attract inferior salaries, you are really a Medical Laboratory Technologist."

After working as a technologist for some years I was told: "Medical Laboratory Technologists are rather inferior sort of persons who attract inferior salaries, you ought to be paid on the same scale as scientific officers in the scientific civil service. You are really a Medical Laboratory Scientific Officer or MLSO."

Dr Tom Hughes-Davies, of whom more later, has since explained to me that it was a time when salaries were frozen and the only way to get a higher one was to become a 'something else'. Dr

Hughes-Davies was an Oxford-trained paediatrician who led the Team from 1969 until it finished early in 1971. Pay parity with the scientific civil service did not last very long, so was it worth changing the name of the profession? State registration was later imposed by the government. I was still an MLSO, state registered, when I retired, but I believe that if I had continued in the service I would have become a bio-medical scientist. Writing in an essay I once stated that I thought the profession just had an unstable nomenclature. In the margin was written 'don't be facetious' and the essay was marked down. It should have been marked up: I was quite right.

The Vietnam job had been advertised in the Institute of Medical Laboratory Science Gazette and I had thought perhaps I ought to apply for it. With my usual procrastination I had not done anything about it until I heard that Dr Joan Guy, a Southampton haematologist, was looking for someone to go to Vietnam. She said that the job with her was the same as the one I had seen advertised in the Gazette. I applied for it unsuccessfully. The letter from the Ministry for Overseas Development said that the post was already filled. (It was later renamed the Overseas Development Administration or ODA and I saw this as downgrading, although I am sure that this had nothing to do with the subsequent activities of the British Medical Team.)

When I told Dr Guy that the post had been filled, she said:

"Oh yes! They've given it to some wretched girl, I'll go and have a row with them."

I thanked her but thought: "Well, you may be big beer in Southampton but you won't cut much ice with the Ministry for Overseas Development."

To my surprise a letter arrived saying the post was once again vacant and would I like to reapply. As it transpired, I got the job because the other applicant had withdrawn. Reconciled with her fiancé she did not want to go to Vietnam after all.

I sat on the plane flying out to Vietnam and wondered what I had done.

"If you had just kept your head down," I thought to myself, "you could be safe in Southampton where at the very worst life might be a little dull." I was, and am, a moral and physical coward and here was I flying into trouble of my own asking.

The plane stopped off in Bahrain at 2am. I wandered over to the transit lounge and was intrigued to see the windows all steamed up - on the outside; it took some thinking about! Once inside, I noticed that the duty-free booze cost a lot less in Dinars than it did in pounds. I had always thought that sterling was the heaviest currency. Wrong again! Dinar comes from the Latin Denarius as does the *d* of £.s.d. (This was before decimalisation.) Of course in our care the *d* has devalued to the point of disappearance.

The Ministry for Overseas Development unloaded the Team onto the Foreign and Commonwealth Office and they unloaded us onto the British Embassy in Saigon. I was told that it was the quickest and easiest way to get us installed. We were termed Embassy Attached. I had never before met and mixed with diplomats or their like.

In Vietnam I discovered that the fifteen or so nurses in the British Medical Team were chosen from a waiting list of four hundred. In other words, they were a highly select bunch to work with; no getting the job because the only other applicant had withdrawn. However, the Ministry for Overseas Development still managed to appoint one or two nurses who were well-qualified for working in the UK but totally unsuited to the peculiar conditions of Vietnam. One of them was an only child and had never been away from home. I can only suppose that the nurses and other members of the Team were appointed on the basis of a letter of application plus an interview, as I was. I became aware that it was a team only by virtue of having arrived at the same place, not of having come from the same place. No one in the Team, before arriving in Vietnam, knew more than one or two of the others.

My motives were first a curiosity about a situation so much in the news, secondly a desire to travel and thirdly, a desire to

7

help without having to take sides. In retrospect, I realise that I also wanted to test and expand my professional skills. I had thought, as anyone would, about how my skills and motives would fit the situation abroad. One will almost certainly wrongly anticipate much of the situation and should not compound any mismatch by deceiving oneself about one's motives. Even now I distrust what people say about why they want to work abroad.

Since then, it has been pointed out to me that many of the Team were escaping from an unsatisfactory situation at home. Looking back, I can see that it was true for some of them but I don't feel that it was particularly so in my case. In Vietnam there was a shortfall between what could be done and what should be done by us, owing to many cultural, climatic, linguistic and logistic problems. My understanding was that the Vietnamese hospital staff had not actually invited us. There is nothing wrong with having the idea of doing good but it must be tempered with a flexible approach as to how. Some of the British Medical Team went home early, frustrated because they had been unable to bridge the gap between what they expected to achieve and what they could actually do.

Self, Mr Mau and colleagues at the coffee stall over the road from the hospital. We had just finished our Phở, a soup which is part of the national diet, served with noodles, 'greenery' and the famous fish sauce called nước mắm.

Pathologist and haematologist Dr Joan Guy, without whom I would not have travelled to Vietnam.

The British Embassy building, Saigon, viewed from the entrance of the Protestant Church.

Right: Saigon Cathedral.
Cables were a feature throughout Saigon.

The traffic and pollution were particularly bad in Saigon.
The fogging in the picture is actually exhaust smoke from two-stroke motor cyclos.

CHAPTER 2

MISCONCEPTIONS AND TURMOIL

Going to Vietnam 'to get some shooting at the weekends' was a story spread by Ray Berry, a Southampton biochemist with a strong sense of drama. Ray also managed to create one or two other myths about 'Martin', which astonished me when I eventually returned. I should explain that we were in Vietnam as civilians. Australia and New Zealand had troops in Vietnam as well as civilian medical teams. Britain had no fighting troops in Vietnam and, I thought at the time, was on the peacekeeping commission together with Poland and India. I thought wrong! Britain was not on the peacekeeping commission.

So that you can learn from these anecdotes, I will leave in the one or two - well, actually more than one or two - things that I got wrong. The Ministry for Overseas Development said that the instructions for embassies abroad indicated that Vietnamese was too difficult to learn, but they could offer me a course in French. By now I was anxious to get to Vietnam. Dr Guy wanted me to arrive before the end of her six-month contract. My first mistake was to decline the French course, which would have delayed my arrival. Later, one of the Embassy staff told me what an excellent course it was. I had left school with not much French, little Latin and less Greek. I had booked a holiday in the Norwegian Jotenheimen with the Wessex Mountaineering Club and I was encouraged to take this holiday to prepare me for life in the tropics. I enjoyed it and it was the right thing to do.

Vietnam was a bit of a cultural and dietary shock. Climatic too. At Saigon's Tan Sơn Nhất airport, leaving the plane was like getting into a sun-warmed car. The smell was different, of course, - slightly earthy with a hint of excrement. I was met at the airport by a couple from the Embassy, David and Fenella Wood. Fenella's family were friends of my parents. I stayed with the Woods for a few days and they eased me into the local milieu. David Wood took me into town to buy shirts; I had not understood that my air freight would take some days to arrive and in a hot and sweaty climate one needed many changes of shirt.

David introduced me to many Embassy staff whose names and functions I almost immediately forgot. His especial job was Embassy liaison with the British Medical Team. David also took me to the Embassy staff residence's swimming pool. In a hot sticky climate a pool is a most wonderful place. I was lucky to be met at Tan Sơn Nhất by the Woods unlike Dr John Clarke who had arrived at the weekend and found his own way by taxi from the airport to the Children's Hospital where the British Medical Team was supposedly working. There he found no Team members or indeed any 'round eyes' (local slang for Westerner or Caucasian) on duty. After a long flight to a country where one doesn't speak the language this is the last sort of problem one wants.

After a few days at the Woods', the Embassy put me in a house with Gerry Chavasse. This was a detached building in the suburbs of Saigon. Two servants came with the house and were expected to stay there when Embassy staff were rotated to other posts. Gerry was to become Information Officer at the Embassy, when he had learned Vietnamese. He had been tested and confirmed to have an ability to learn languages. He did learn Vietnamese and was later reported in the Vietnamese press as accompanying the Ambassador on various official visits. However, I could never understand his French; perhaps it was just too good.

Gerry's ambition was to split the morpheme, the linguist's equivalent of splitting the atom. Perhaps he was looking for an expletive release of energy. The morpheme is the smallest unit of meaningful language. He also wanted to find out why the

Vietnamese often called the Americans '*Meos*'. *Meo* is the Vietnamese for cat. He said: "I asked the Vietnamese and then I listened for the silence, but there was no particular silence, they just said that they did not know."

Years later I now know that it probably comes from the Chinese word for America, *Mei*. The usual Vietnamese word for America is *My* which also means grain. *My* in Chinese means cooked rice.

Gerry told me how in the weeks before the lunar New Year festival of Tet 1968, there had been a lot of funerals in Saigon, of people from the countryside. At Tet the Viet Cong simultaneously attacked Saigon and every major city in South Vietnam. All this had taken place a few months before I arrived. The Viet Cong had infiltrated themselves into Saigon, exhumed their 'dead relatives' and extracted the AK 47 rifles from the coffins. They almost succeeded in taking over the city and had penetrated the American Embassy ground floor. The cemeteries in Saigon were surrounded by seven foot high walls and were not generally overlooked, so there was plenty of cover for any diggings up and assembly of weapons. The Viet Cong knew that initially their gunfire would be taken as the traditional New Year firecrackers.

The British Embassy was half a mile down the road from the President's palace. There were deer in the palace grounds. The Embassy's Gurkha guards said that when the palace was attacked both the guards and the deer ran away and by the time they reached the British Embassy the palace guards were in front of the deer. It was not understood at the time that the Viet Cong were nearly wiped out during Tet. When a few years later Saigon fell it was to the NVA, the North Vietnamese Army, not the Viet Cong guerrillas.

I originally wrote that my friends the Woods had sat behind their seven-foot high wall hearing the gun fire and listening to the BBC World Service to find out what was going on outside their gates. After I sent a copy of this essay to David Wood and Fenella, they sent me the following e-mail, to put me right about Tet and one or two other things.

"I think you may have bought in a bit too readily to the cynical idea that the team was simply a political ploy, and did not need to do anything beyond being there; as Barbara Evans in Caduceus...makes clear, there was a real humanitarian motivation to the concept, reinforced by the rapid deployment of the refugee relief team after the Tet offensive. It was never going to be easy for the team to work in the Vietnamese environment in Nhi Dong: from outside, it was always impressive how much the team did what they could, sought out ways to be of service, and saw problems as there to be dealt with.

Who was Dr Bass? We don't remember him and his colourful but, we would argue, skewed picture. UK was not a member of the International Control Commission set up to monitor the 1954 partition agreement (these were India, Poland and Canada), but was a Co-Chairman of the Geneva Conference with Russia! The US never signed the Geneva agreements, and only got some support from SEATO members for its contention that a threat to Vietnamese integrity amounted to an attack on the US itself - hence its military involvement.

The UK resisted any suggestion of putting troops into VN, but supported the RVN with our aid programme (which was always separate from military assistance) and advice on counter-insurgency, drawing on our experience in Malaya provided in your and our time by the 'Police Advisers' but originally by Sir Robert Thompson himself. Lots of background analysis in Brian Crozier's book *Turmoil in South East Asia*.

You are not right about us on the night of the Tet offensive. There is actually a better story! We slept through the night, only remarking the loudness of what we took as firecrackers. So in the morning, discounting our maid's "much shooting last night: many people die...", David set off to use the holiday to catch up on work in the office. The roads were eerily quiet, and the Mini was stopped by military police at a barrier by the US Embassy. Having argued his way past, he noted the rocket hole blasted in the front of the building, passed the barrier at the other end, and arrived at our Embassy, diagonally across the road, to find the security guards and one or two others in the lobby, the ground floor window glass shattered, and the Gurkhas in their quarters where they had been shepherded when the fighting started - to prevent them joining in! He then drove warily home where we endured the, initially 24-hour, curfew. It was that evening when we sat in our bungalow unable to see out, trying to interpret what was going on from the sounds of helicopters turning overhead, and tanks firing along the road in what turned out to be clearing out the nearby local cemetery of Viet Cong! (We can't vouch for the deer/palace guards story, I'm afraid)."

After Tet 1968, refugees poured into the Saigon area and camps for them were hurriedly set up. The Paediatric team was expanded in haste, from fourteen or so to twenty-seven, so that we could give medical help to these camps. The expanded team needed more transport and the Embassy somehow scrounged three ex-army Land Rovers from Singapore. These were painted grey and had red crosses over their original army green. By the time I arrived in October 1968 the refugee problem was diminishing and the team beginning to contract.

A motor cyclo used as a furniture van.

CHAPTER 3

ACCLIMATISING

At my briefing in London, I'd asked if it was possible to cycle in Saigon. I'd been told very firmly: "No, it is not possible to cycle in Saigon."

This rather surprised me, as I thought the indigenous people did cycle. When I arrived I saw the local people cycling while I sat like Lord Muck in the long-wheelbase Land Rover chauffeured by Ong Hai, the local Team driver. Being chauffeured was not the luxury it seemed; it used to lose me most of my lunch hour. The Ministry for Overseas Development would have been happy to ship out a new British car for me but at that time MLSOs could not generally afford to drive. Later they reluctantly shipped out my bicycle and I was then far more mobile and had time to get a swim in at lunchtime. A Team Land Rover became available soon after the bicycle arrived and I could give people lifts, or even travel out of town when permitted by the Embassy.

Two factors produced a horrendous traffic situation in Saigon. Firstly, economic experts had said that, with so much American money coming into the country, if there were nothing to buy there would be high inflation. A large number of Honda 49cc motorcycles were imported. A popular story said that the Honda company had given ten thousand Hondas to the national police force to popularise them. Any motorcycle became a 'Xe Honda'. Xe is the classifier for almost any type of wheeled vehicle. A motorcycle of less than 50cc did not require a driving licence under the old French law. Secondly, the idea of smooth laminar traffic flow, or slower traffic keeping nearer the side of the road, is completely absent from the Vietnamese psyche. It is, of course, so fundamental to our way of thinking that we don't think about it. I had a lot of accidents, not all of them minor.

I was soon introduced to Dr John Bass, whose nutrition was entirely liquid, or so I was told; we could get duty free booze from the Embassy Commissary. Dr Bass was from South Africa and I never really understood how he fitted into the Team. Originally he had been billeted with a Defence Attaché, Colonel Varwell, but their life styles were different, the pairing did not work and the Colonel requested a change. Dr Mike Inman, the first Team anaesthetist moved in with Colonel Varwell and they remained lifelong friends. In the meantime, Dr Bass was transferred to a house in Công Lý, where he became a problem for Dr Bill Collis.

According to Bill, he had been asleep, when well after midnight the servant girl had hammered on his bedroom door saying: "Monsieur, Monsieur. Much police militar." (The Vietnamese police were called 'White Mice' and American military police, who wore white helmets, were called 'Snow Drops'.)

Bill had gone downstairs in his dressing gown to find Dr Bass and two American civilians at one side of the room confronted by numerous 'White Mice' and 'Snow Drops' on the other side. The combined squad had pursued Dr Bass the length of Công Lý and up the cul-de-sac into the house. They wanted to arrest Dr Bass and his cronies. Bill at this point could not help and went back to bed. He believes that Dr Bass and his cronies were taken away by the police, though Dr Bass did come back next morning, only to be sacked soon after by the Embassy who had had enough.

It was Dr Bass who told me his version of how a British Medical Team came to be in Saigon. Apparently it was all due to the Americans. The Americans had said to the British: "We are spending a million dollars a day in Vietnam, what are you British doing?" The British Government of the day, quite spontaneously, decided that perhaps under the Colombo Plan, they would like to offer medical aid to both North and South Vietnam so as to be fair.

The North Vietnamese said: "Don't send a team, because we don't want them to see what our regime is really like, but we would like any medicines that you care to send."

The South Vietnamese response was: "Oh, if you must send a medical team, put it in the Children's Hospital. It is the most corrupt and ill-administered hospital in Vietnam, and it doesn't already have an American team."

So the British Medical Team was sent to Bệnh-Viện Nhi-Đồng, the Saigon children's hospital. The Vietnamese Minister of Health rang up the director, Dr Tuan, and said: "Oh, by the way you are having a British medical team installed at your hospital, and you had better find them an office for their tea breaks and coffee making."

Dr Bass explained that just being in Vietnam fulfilled our political purpose. He recommended I did not bother with work but just enjoyed myself. Well, I did try to do some work, but as a start I had to adjust to the peculiar climate and situation.

When the Embassy put me in a house, I would find a servant already installed and I would have to take over paying her when the previous occupant left; it was always a 'her' in Vietnam. The bigger houses used by the Embassy had two or three servants. I was told three things about servants. Firstly, servants had to be either ethnic Chinese or Vietnamese but not both as they did not mix in the same household. Mind you, I could not tell the difference, but this hardly mattered as I never had more than one servant at a time. Secondly, Vietnamese were either South Vietnamese or refugees from the North who had voted against Communism with their feet and there was some tension between them. We thought that the North Vietnamese were more hard working and enterprising. The South Vietnamese thought that the North Vietnamese were just better at sweet-talking the boss. The third thing that had to be taken into account was inflation. The value of money halved every year or eighteen months so servants really did need regular pay rises.

I'd never run a house with a servant. It was a completely new experience, and I didn't really do it well either, but that's by the way. Of course, the first thing I had asked was if it was really necessary to have a servant. It was! Servants prevented burglary while one was at work and could buy food at better prices. They gave one an entry into the Vietnamese way of thinking. There were no washing machines or launderettes (coin-ops) out there. The idea of employing a servant should not be condemned out of hand by those who do not understand the situation. Or, to put it another way: "It is the duty of the wealthy man to give employment to the artisan."

I have seen a South African lady lambasted because she happened to mention having a servant. I tried to explain to her English attackers, without success, that it might actually be good to employ servants in South Africa. Applying English values to a foreign situation was bad manners and usually bad judgement.

On my arrival at the laboratory, Dr Guy said: "I have told them all how absolutely marvellous you are. Please don't let me down."

I never really knew what she had said about me, but many years later I discovered what she really thought: not much! The trouble was that I had limitations. I still have. At my original briefing by the Ministry for Overseas Development, I'd asked the obvious questions like: "Will I be in charge?"

"No!"

"Whom am I working for?"

"You are working for the South Vietnamese Ministry of Health."

"Who pays my salary?"

"The British taxpayer."

"Right, if I'm not in charge, and I'm being paid by the British taxpayer, what do I have to do?"

At this point they said that I was there…"to set a good example."

How do you set a good example in the laboratory? Setting a bad example would, of course, have been easy. Although all this left me not knowing what on earth I was supposed to do, I was in fact better briefed than many of the nurses who had been told exactly, and wrongly, what they were supposed to do.

In other words, the Ministry had wised up by the time they got to me. The story goes that there was an Australian radiographer who had been told that he was in charge by the Australian Government or somebody far away. The Vietnamese didn't like him bossing them around and they buggered off and left him on his own for three days. Apparently by the time he had run the X-ray department single-handed for three days he was much more polite. Some of the nurses ended up neither nursing, nor in charge, contrary to what they had been told, but teaching English to their Vietnamese colleagues.

Much local life took place on the streets. This is a Honda motorcycle side walk repair service, operated by boys because so many of the men were in the army. Vietnam had more under 25s than over 25s...

Arc welding a grill on the pavement.

A cyclo (or xích lô)
- a familiar sight.

The taxis were always
French Quatre Chevaux.

Five a side! Lambro bus.

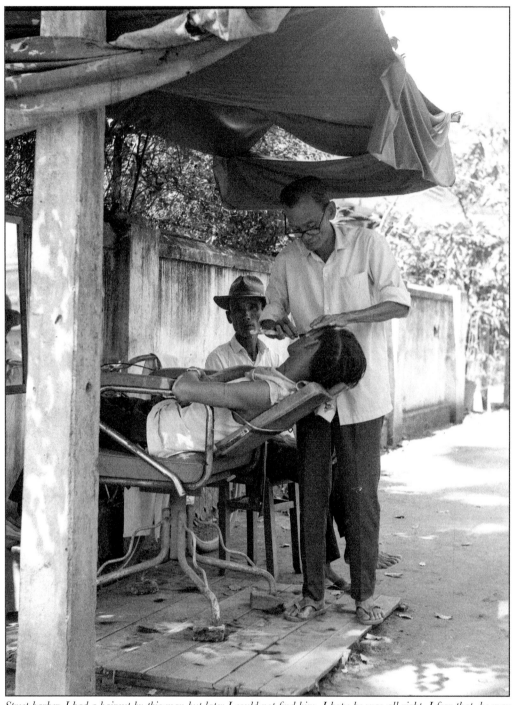

Street barber. I had a haircut by this man but later I could not find him. I hope he was all right. I fear that, he may have been hounded out of business by 'cowboys' (gangsters and draft dodgers) or 'White Mice' (the police). He is shaving this customer's eyebrows. This is not recommended, as eyebrows do not always grow back.

26

Top: A Lambro bus and a Honda have come to grief.
Above: The bus and Honda, now righted by the policeman and a passer-by. The bus driver's toolbox is by his feet.

Main railway line out of Saigon. The trains were infrequent!

Some of the lab. staff. Standing at the left: Dược Sĩ Anh. Back row, left to right: Malcolm Wright, the Team anaesthetist, the top of Mr Mau's head, Dr Hughes-Davies, Team leader, Dr Pool. One of our nurses, the late Tessa Gray and our Vietnamese administrator, Ong Luan.

Front row: Three new technicians, Monsieur Tam with a cigarette, Susan Wright and the alluring Co Ut.

Dr Douglas Stanley, the British pathologist, had co-opted Malcolm Wright's wife Susan to help start the histology service. Susan had accompanied Malcolm to Vietnam. She turned out to have a useful degree in pharmacology. I think that it must have been Dr Stanley who took the photograph, as he is not in it.

One day Monsieur Tam had told me that they had applied to the School of Pharmacy for twenty new technicians. I said: 'Too many! Three would be about right.' He said: 'We apply for twenty and we will get three.' We didn't get three we got twenty! I think the three in the front row might have been from the twenty. I never did know their names.

CHAPTER 4

TEAM SPIRIT AND TALENTS

One of my mistakes was to be the wrong sex: I don't feel guilty about it. The idea had been that the Team pathology technician, or technologist, or MLSO, by whatever name, would be a woman who could decently share a house with Mrs Peta Andrea, the radiographer. Instead I was used by the Embassy as a sort of caretaker. If the Embassy had managed to rent a house or flat they didn't like to let it go, and they found it quite useful to use me to hold it down. I spent time in about twelve different houses or flats during the two years or so in Vietnam.

Mrs Andrea was extremely hospitable. I used a Team Land Rover to drive her to the American PX (Post Exchange) to buy great supplies of food and drink. One evening she was entertaining one or two people, including a rather fat American colonel, who asked me how I managed to stay slim. I was fairly drunk at the time and so it came to me instantly that the secret of staying slim was to employ a bad cook like the one I had, and not go round to Mrs Andrea's too often.

One of the various people concerned with the British Medical Team was Mr Luan, or Ong Luan, to give him his Vietnamese title. He was said to be the best nurse anaesthetist in South Vietnam. When he became administrator for the British Medical Team he no longer gave anaesthetics, but then he was a good administrator. If you wanted your bicycle repaired, or had lost your key or wanted paper for making decorations, you went to Mr Luan and he could always help, and very often at no expense.

David Wood handled liaison between Team and Embassy. Later this job passed to Mark Pellew who said: "I can't understand why the British Medical Team can't see through Mr Luan…" implying that Mr Luan was dishonest. As far as I know Mr Luan was honest, though he probably did take some commission on the things that he handled.

The nurses were an intelligent and spirited lot. In spite of their intelligence they failed to grasp the well-known fact that Vietnamese is more or less impossible to learn. They worked mornings only for the first fortnight, and in the afternoons had Vietnamese lessons. With these lessons and what they picked up on the wards many of them became fairly fluent. One of the nurses, Sylvia Ferns, was fluent enough to understand indirect speech. She was something of a singer which helped her as Vietnamese is a tonal language. I'm told by one of the other nurses that Sylvia had a bent for the language right from the word go and could even get the tones right.

Some of the nurses were invited into upper class Vietnamese homes. Sylvia's Vietnamese was apparently of the demotic sort, having been learned on the wards. I was told the Vietnamese who understood the situation were amused by it.

I invited Sylvia to dinner one evening and gave her roast lamb. We could get excellent New Zealand lamb from the British Embassy Commissary. Now I had to apologise to Sylvia for having no mint sauce for the lamb. She said: "In my house we always have a mint sauce." So she got on my phone, rang up the house where she was billeted and spoke to her servant in Vietnamese. We had my servant speak to her servant on the phone.

My servant's boy friend, Dan Ong, popped out to the local soup seller's barrow, within hearing range of the house, and came back in less than a minute with mint; Dan Ong comes into the story again later. Soup sellers and other itinerant tradesmen had their particular street cries and sounds. One heard them coming like modern ice cream vans. I even have their cries on tape.

Dr Joan Guy wanted me in the laboratory as soon as possible and I never had the initial start in Vietnamese. Dr Guy said that anyone who was anyone spoke French anyway. While this was true of her doctor colleagues it was not true of more junior staff, let alone 'the polloi' (or 'hoi polloi' as we say). Dr Guy was on a six-month contract and three months had gone before I got to Vietnam, so I only overlapped with her for three months. She said that she'd sorted out the haematology in the lab, and would I look after the chemistry, which I tried to do. The first British pathologist, a Dr Young, had set up the laboratory and had it built with British funds. It had air conditioning, quite a good supply of chemicals, basic microscopes and four Coleman Junior spectrophotometers, of which more later.

I never heard the full story about Dr Young; the gist of it seems to be that, having achieved a lot in spite of the difficulties, he retired sick. His Vietnamese deputy, Dr Nguyen, who was incredibly intelligent, spoke quite good English, French, Vietnamese and could read Chinese, asked me to write to Dr Young.

Letters to and from the Saigon British Embassy went by BFPO, as had letters to me in Cyprus during my National Service. Letters through the BFPO (British Forces Post Office) and British Post Office did get through, so I was puzzled to get no reply to the one I wrote. I thought at the time, that perhaps Dr Young did not want anything more to do with his Vietnamese colleague. Letters through the Vietnamese PTT did not always arrive as the PTT workers sometimes stole the stamps. On a 1996 package tour of Vietnam, we were still advised to get our mail franked rather than use stamps if we wanted our post cards to arrive in the UK.

There was another Dr Young, the Ministry of Health (*Bo-Y-Te*)'s Dr Wang Tsio Young who fronted the liaison with the foreign medical team's committee. I have found out since then that our Dr Young did not reply because he really was very ill.

Pharmacists (*Dược Sĩ*) ran the hospital laboratories in Vietnam. This seemed odd to us. *Dược Sĩ* could prescribe and treat independently of doctors. We were rather against this system, partly because our pharmacist, Dược Sĩ Anh, seemed to have been appointed for whom he knew, rather than what he knew.

He could not speak English and his French was not too good, so we tended to ignore him, even when he did come in to work. The Vietnamese had learned one or two tricks from the French. When Dr Joan Guy or somebody complained that things were not so wonderful as they ought to be, the Vietnamese would keep quiet for a day or two and then, when we arrived in the laboratory, they said: "Right, well, we've changed everything."

There would be a big blackboard, with squares and arrows on it, and in the squares would be the names of the various people, and the arrows would point down the ladder of seniority, and they'd say: "Right, well now, Mr Tam is in charge, and Dược Sĩ Anh is deputy to Dr Nguyen, and everything is completely changed." Of course, it was only a diagram on a blackboard and nothing had changed at all: good army-style bullshit! In retrospect I think that maybe this was the best way to handle Dr Joan Guy who was inclined to be a bit fierce.

Monsieur Tam in the lab.

Fenella Wood and right, Mrs Peta Andrea, enjoying life around the Embassy pool.

The new lift tower under construction. Note the extreme economy of materials. The roof slab has an upturned side and is not nearly as thick as it looks in the photograph but then frost damage to concrete can be ruled out in such a warm climate. The columns are somewhat slender and the recycled wood scaffolding rickety beyond belief. I would like to know how this delicate structure has fared over the last forty years. The materials hoist at the top (pictured right) is made from an army telephone cable drum.

A greeting of rubbish, some of a medical nature, in the street by the entrance to Nhi Đồng.

Bệnh-Viện Nhi-Đồng West Wing, built by the French.

A dinner at the lab. Sometimes we provided turkey from the American Post Exchange (PX), the equivalent of the British NAAFI, as our contribution to the meal. That way we did not have to eat pig's trachea or dog meat and be polite about it. (I'm on the right, with the beard.)

A graduation dinner at the School of Pharmacy; note the salvaged flare parachute sunshades.

CHAPTER 5

TECHNOLOGY SAIGON STYLE

At the Saigon School of Medical Laboratory Technology, the technicians got a good grounding in theory but not in practice. Some strange things happened.

I kept odds and ends in an old antibiotic test paper tin. These test papers are little spider-shaped things and each leg of the spider has a different antibiotic on it. You put your paper spider on the surface of the petri plate and watched where the bacteria grew; from the wound or throat swab or whatever. If the growth was inhibited round one of the legs of the spider you knew the bug was sensitive to that antibiotic. The Vietnamese saw this tin and were amazed: "Six antibiotics in one formulation! We have no medicine like this in Vietnam!"

Dr Duncan McCauley, the newly arrived Team leader, persuaded Janice Edmondson, who had been in the country quite a long time, to guide us to the Buddhist orphanage at Go Vap. It was clean and well-organised and made a point of welcoming visitors of all nationalities. I think this was to attract funds. Janice and several of the other nurses in the team knew Go Vap well. There were other orphanages in the Saigon area, but I suspect they were not as impressive.

With not one colleague to call on for help, I had to know everything from autoclaves to the Ziehl-Neelsen technique. I was unable to mend the ultraviolet spectrophotometer, which meant that we could never do Glucose 6 Phosphate De-hydrogenases.

Don't ask what G6PDs are, I have long forgotten. Even after ten years in the Southampton laboratories, there were gaps in my knowledge - probably more gaps than knowledge. Another trouble was the supply lines were too long. The Crown Agents took fourteen months to supply a new haematocrit centrifuge. I became expert in reshaping car dynamo brushes to fit centrifuges and replacing the fuse-able links in the autoclave with solder wire. It did not help to have very few textbooks.

In one respect I was lucky. When I trained I was circulated through all departments in the laboratory so as to get an outline knowledge of all the disciplines, these being bacteriology, histology, haematology, and chemistry. This system was abandoned probably about the time labs started accepting degree entry. I had achieved Fellowship of the Institute of Medical Laboratory Science. It had been the Institute of Medical Laboratory Technology but like the Overseas Development Administration it had changed title. In those days, to get Fellowship, you had to study a second discipline, and my disciplines were chemistry and bacteriology.

Because of the demands of the laboratory in Southampton, I'd also done quite a lot of haematology at the junior level. In those days, the haematology department also had to take blood on wards and in the outpatient department, and consequently needed a lot of staff. One stayed longer in the haematology department. Of course I was not qualified to diagnose disease, and I was weak on blood banking and coagulation. However, I did know what a normal blood film looked like and could easily get local expert help to identify the different malarias.

I was also lucky to have physics 'A' level which helped me to work things out from first principles. The electricity supply was a nominal 110 volts, but often less. However 220 volt equipment could often be wired 'across the phases' as many houses had a three phase supply. A consequence of this was that our lights in the living room could go out while the lights, on a different phase, in the servant's quarters would stay on. I thought this a bit of a swindle. Most houses had an autotransformer about the size of a coal scuttle; a very heavy coal scuttle I should add. If the lights went dim, or the air conditioner shuddered to a halt, one turned the transformer up a notch. This worked until too many other neighbours did the same and brought down the supply altogether.

We had knife switches for the lights. They looked a hundred years out of date but worked quite well. After thinking from first principles, I decided that they were safer than our switches as they were double pole, adequately shrouded and one could see at a glance if a switch was on or off. In the lab, our three kilowatt British water baths (*Bain Marie*), at 110 volts, took alarmingly high currents from the slender two-pin French-style sockets.

Mrs Andrea was friendly with the Dutch consul and, through her, I came to speak to the architect for the school the Dutch were building. He put it to me that 110 volts was dangerous. I asked him why as I thought the risk of fatal shock was far less at 110 volts. He pointed out to me that the fire risk was that much greater due to the heavy currents needed.

The water supply was also low voltage, so to speak. My house in Phan Đinh Phùng needed an electric pump to get the water from street level to my bathroom on the first floor.

One of my jobs was to go to the (I think it was the 9th) American Field Hospital and scrounge their time-expired blood. As I remember, the Americans worked to a twenty-one day time limit, and the Vietnamese considered that the American blood could be used for a further fortnight. The theory then was: a red blood cell was supposed to have a lifetime in the body, or in storage, of about one hundred days. If you took blood from somebody, some of the cells were new (in other words they had one hundred days to go) while some of the cells were at the end of their hundred days, but on average they'd got fifty days to go.

If you give blood to somebody after twenty-five days storage, half of it is used up and breaks down rapidly when given to a patient. In other words, it can do more harm than good. The American and Vietnamese ABO blood group frequencies did not match very well and we sometimes had too much of one group and always not enough of another. The Vietnamese were said to be all Rhesus positive; I hope they really were, as we did not do Rhesus grouping.

There was an existing blood transfusion service, at any rate in Saigon, if not in the provinces. We in the medical team were doubtful about how good it was.

One day, Dr Malcolm Wright came into the lab and said: "Please can I use your haematocrit centrifuge?"

He then said: "The child's haematocrit is 27 per cent and the blood donor's is only 17 per cent. Should the patient's blood be used to transfuse the donor?"

A person who is not anaemic has a haematocrit of about 45 per cent. The child's haematocrit, at 27 per cent, was about two-thirds of what it should have been; definitely anaemic. It was the donor who had the real problem!

Is a paid blood donor service really such a good idea? Our blood donor service picked up that my blood donor friend Fred Fouch was anaemic. As a result he was diagnosed early and treated vigorously for leukaemia. He lived to get his children through school and into jobs and die of something else. He attributed his cure to Dr Bamforth and a haematologist at Southampton, Dr Hyde. When Fred died, I wrote to Dr Hyde who told me that the next five patients, treated the same way as Fred, had died. Leukaemia cures were not common in those days.

A nun explaining to Dr McCauley how the orphanage water was siphoned from the top jars through 'filter candles' into the bottom jars to make it safe to drink. A filter candle is an unglazed earthenware tube with pores small enough to stop bacteria getting through. Viruses, however, can get through.

The reception hut at Go Vap Orphanage. Note the flags of 'The Free World'.

This little Buddhist shrine was given to the hospital by the builder of the new laboratory wing and lift tower.

Orphans two to each cot. They were clean but probably did not get a lot of TLC. I wonder what sort of people they have grown up to be.

Below: A side street.

The Refectory at Go Vap Orphanage. The furniture and structure was made from old packing cases.
The Vietnamese were very good at reusing materials.

CHAPTER 6

PRIVILEGES AND FINANCES

We had American PX privileges. The PX, or Post Exchange, was equivalent to the British Armed Services NAAFI. You could buy anything from baked beans to jock straps.

Dr Mike Inman, after his time as British Medical Team anaesthetist, went to work for the Americans. He convinced the Americans that we should have access to the PX as the Americans would have had to put a medical team into the hospital if there hadn't been a British one there.

Payment in the PX was not made in US dollars or in Vietnamese currency, the Dong, but in Military Payment Certificates - MPCs (or red dollars). At first we had no official way of getting MPCs but were officially allowed to spend them. By the time I arrived there was a proper supply exchange system.

Now the Americans could, and did, change the issue of MPCs. One night the issue 680 changed to issue 681, and we all had to go to offices in the American bases and exchange our 680 MPCs for 681s. The Vietnamese government were said to have lost a substantial unofficial holding of 680 issue MPCs. The changes of issue of MPCs were meant to frustrate black marketeers and pimps and to isolate the local economy from the inflationary effect of large amounts of American money coming into circulation.

Money was much more complicated than just Dongs and Dollars, both red and green, and Pounds and Piastres. With steady inflation the Dong lost about half its value every year or eighteen months.

I asked Dr Nguyen, the Vietnamese pathologist, about his mortgage. He told me that his repayments were equivalent to about three English pounds a month. This was easily affordable even on his minute salary. M.Tam, the chief technician, lived in quite a modest house but when he counted up its value he realised that he was a Dong millionaire. On returning to the UK in 1971 I found people unaware that inflation here had crept up to significant levels. I bought a house as quickly as I could!

The official name for the Dong was Piastre which was written VN$. In an effort to control inflation the Vietnamese government had set up two different exchange rates for the Piastre. The diplomatic exchange rate which the Embassy had to use was something like 100 VN$ to the £, the official ordinary or tourist rate perhaps 200 VN$ to the £. There was also the black market rate equivalent to about 350 VN$ to the pound when the pound had been converted into US$.

The black marketeers really preferred dollars to sterling. Co-incidentally at the time, a pound was worth about US$2.4. This made a US cent exactly the same value as one old pence. (£1 = 240 old pence). The Embassy told me quite firmly, not to exchange money on the black market, and I never did. It was said that the gaol sentences for illegal money dealing were proportional to the difference between the official and black market rates of exchange. One of the Team had a friend who cycled money through different currencies in such a way as to end up with more than he started with.

We also had British Embassy Commissary privileges, which were most useful as we were able to get excellent New Zealand lamb, butter, beer and tinned goods, including evaporated milk. Fruit and vegetables came from the local market. I learned just enough Vietnamese to ask Chi Hai (or Sister Two, the number One of the house being me, of course, and the Two, the servant): "Tomorrow go market buy…." at the end of which sentence I could substitute various fruit and vegetables or French bread, delicious with butter from the Commissary.

The diplomats had to entertain as part of their job, so there was a really wonderful selection of wines, sherries and spirits available, all duty free. I was able to experiment with drinks which I'd never been able to afford or been inclined to try before. I found that it was true that one shouldn't drink before sundown, not so much because it causes the decline of the British Empire but because it makes the afternoon's work such a drag.

Vietnam, China and Japan are non-milk cultures. I could not get any milk until I was given access to the PX and Embassy Commissary. I really missed my milk. The PX milk was reconstituted, in Vietnam, from imported skimmed dried milk and coconut fat. Our administrator, Mr Luan had a stomach ulcer and Dr Hughes-Davies had advised him to drink milk. Mr Luan asked me if milk gave me diarrhoea and I told him it didn't. I did not understand at the time that almost all adults in non-milk cultures are lactose intolerant. I was surprised during my last few months in Vietnam to find small pots of locally-made yoghurt, no doubt with the lactose fermented out. I don't know where the milk came from - probably imported tinned milk.

Pool parties at the Embassy sometimes involved Scottish dancing.
Second from left, Colonel Varwell. In the flowered dress, Jean Hicks from the British
Medical Team.

CHAPTER 7

FITTING IN...

At Bệnh-Viện Nhi-Đồng, I found myself dropped into an already working laboratory. I saw it as my job to find out what they were doing, and where I could fit in or help. I was a newly-qualified technician and I could not communicate with two-thirds of the staff in their own language. In other words, I was a bit lost. Dr Bác Sĩ Hoang Khai Nguyen, the Vietnamese pathologist, spoke good English and was most helpful; this was before he was whisked off to America.

I found myself working mostly with Mr Mau, a very bright Vietnamese technician who spoke some English, or Monsieur Tam, an older man with good French (a good deal better than mine). M. Tam told me that the French Ambassador had given him a certificate for his French. M. Tam had been taught 'English' boxing in his youth. Mr Mau and M. Tam were both very patriotic.

I heard years later that when they took over Saigon the Communists arrested Mr Mau. M. Tam, as a Communist, was politically correct and could have helped, but he had died by that time. However, the hospital staff had gone to the authorities and said that Mr Mau was essential to running the laboratory. So Mr Mau had been released after one day in jail, but then had a very tough time for many years and eventually changed his profession from technician to viniculturist and engineer. When I saw him in 1996, he had restored his family fortunes to some extent. He had put his son through medical school and his son was able to control the diabetes that Mr Mau had by then developed.

I think it possible that the British Medical Team gave quite a boost to Embassy social life. There were three famous parties organised by the Team. The first one was at the staff residency's swimming pool, where several people got thrown into the water. There was a great deal of noise, drink and jollity, but no real drunkenness. There was Scottish dancing for those who wanted to do it. Out of doors was as warm as indoors, but dark by only 7pm. I was newly in the country and found it a strange experience.

Later, the filters of the swimming pool were found to be blocked with noodles. A Chinese soup seller with his barrow had been invited into the grounds. The soup was part of the national diet. It was called *phở* pronounced fir. *Phở* actually refers to the noodles which were served in the soup. The soup was always a clear sort of bouillon and it often had mint, and stuff rather like cress, in it. You could lift out the greenery and noodles with your chopsticks and dunk them in the famous fish sauce called *nước mắm*. *Nước* is the Vietnamese classifier for water or fluid and *mắm* is the Vietnamese for a kind of fish, so this was the famous fermented fish sauce; presumably similar to the ancient Roman garum or liquamen.

We were allowed to take two guests to the pool. In our lunch hours I took Mr Mau and Cô Tình from the lab and taught them to swim. Actually I taught Mr Mau to swim while Cô Tình taught herself. I then gave them a lunch of baked beans and French bread. Teaching them to swim may have been the only lasting good that I achieved in Vietnam. As a thank you, Mr Mau and Cô Tình gave me a basket of the best Vietnamese mangos - and they *are* the best in the world.

Mr Mau also arranged a Vietnamese fondue for lunch in my house. An aluminium cone-shaped charcoal brazier was set up on my table. An annular dish was slipped over the cone and came to rest about half way down. This was filled with coconut milk, which soon came to the boil. We dropped shreds of raw beef into the boiling liquid with chopsticks. Mr Mau liked to take them out lightly cooked; I liked to leave mine in a bit longer. We then dipped the beef into 'Special acetic acid made from bananas' in Mr Mau's words, or to us, banana vinegar. To finish the meal we drank the coconut milk, which had turned into soup.

There was another party, which I didn't go to, but it was widely talked about, and that was the Than Lanh party. Than Lanh are the little gecko lizards that eat insects; you find them everywhere east of the Mediterranean. They climb up walls and can run across - or is that under - ceilings, without falling off. There is a slightly larger lizard that has a peculiar cry which sounds just like: 'Fuck you' repeated three times with diminishing intensity. I wrongly attributed the sound to the geckos. The gecko lizards were captured, dressed in racing colours and raced. The memory of this party no doubt lingered long in the legends of the Embassy.

The nurses in one house decided that they would like to celebrate Julius Caesar's birthday and have a Roman orgy type party. This was the third party of great fame. I made Roman architecture out of paper with the help of John Clarke, the very talented team surgeon. He also produced a statue of Bacchus, made of fracture-setting plaster, brandishing an enamel wine mug.

The guests at these parties were all young ex-pats from the British Medical Team, the Embassy, the Bank of Hong Kong and Shanghai and a few others. There was a curfew at 10pm, if I remember correctly. I had driven to this party in a Team Land Rover. I left well after curfew, dressed in a bedsheet as a Roman, and was stopped at a road block. A little Vietnamese with a rifle and a torch came up out of his sandbagged sentry box and shone the torch over the Land Rover and me, absolutely straight-faced, and then waved me on without turning a hair at a 'round eye' wearing a bed sheet.

To digress for a moment from Vietnam. In Southampton I met a square dancer whose husband had been on the Saigon Embassy staff. She spent a long time telling me how horrible the Vietnamese were. Her husband had been out with some people from the Embassy when the radiator of their car had boiled dry. They asked for water and were ignored by the nearby Vietnamese. Enquiring whether the Vietnamese had really understood what her husband had been saying, she replied: "Well, of course, they understood."

I said: "Sometimes one doesn't really talk these languages as well as one thinks."

"No, of course they understood that he wanted water for his radiator," she said, adding: "Well, of course everyone knows the Vietnamese for water is 'nick-nock.'

Water is NOT nick-nock! Water is *nước*. When I say *nước* means water, drinking water would be *nước uống*, tea might be *nước cha*, urine is *nước tiểu*, and, I have already mentioned *nước mắm*, fermented fish sauce. Most interestingly ice is *nước da*, or water-stone. One's country can be described as one's *Nước*.

Jean Hicks, a nurse in the team, once wanted to be photographed carrying a pair of water cans on a yoke and borrowed some from a little old Vietnamese lady. Although tall and sturdy, Jean could hardly get the water cans off the ground! The yoke has to be adjusted to fit the person so that the load can be lifted with a straight back by straightening the knees. My father once mentioned that, in the 1914-18 war, he had seen 'Chinese' coolies in France who had been employed to dig trenches. I wonder if the 'Chinese' coolies might actually have been Vietnamese from French Indo-China.

After my time with Gerry Chavasse, the Embassy put me in a house in a cul-de-sac off Công Lý street. The house came with Tan, the servant girl, a sub-machine gun and a beautiful bougainvillea. When friends of the former residents started visiting I realised that the house also had a history. Dr Collis from the team was still there, but returned to the UK fairly soon after I arrived. When Dr Collis had gone, and I had been on my own for some time, I thought that I ought to do something about the machine gun and the bougainvillea. I pruned the bougainvillea with a kitchen knife (and, by the way, it is very thorny). I asked Tan to get rid of the sub machine gun. Months later an American turned up and asked for his machine gun as he was going to the Delta. Tough titties! I had to ask how had he managed so long without it.

At Công Lý we occasionally received letters addressed to people unknown to us, the Embassy, or the Medical Team. One day I had just left the house when I was intercepted by a rather menacing man who insisted that I return to the house so that he could collect his letters. I was told later that he was thought to be a freelance arms dealer. I wondered which former resident had invited him to use the Công Lý address. Could it have been Dr Bass from South Africa, I wondered. I never did understand how he fitted into the Team.

Our cul-de-sac was relatively quiet. A French family lived near the Công Lý end and their Peugeot car was blown up one night; why or by whom I do not know. A refugee family lived in a hut at the side of the track to the house and kept a pig there. To leave room for cars, the hut and pig sty were only about four foot wide. Street traders came along our cul-de-sac from time to time, each trader with his own cry or sound. The cry "*Caw ah*" is the soup seller. The small bell is the ice man, the knife sharpener has a strap with brass plates and the resonant wood clappers are the sound of the soup seller again.

One evening I came back drunk from a party and there waiting for me at the gate was an irresistible Vietnamese girl who thought she knew me. I knew I did not know her but I invited her in to my bed anyway, despite being too drunk to perform, perhaps fortuitously as it may have saved me from rather nasty gonorrhea. She was not after my money and I could only think that she had liked one of the Team and genuinely thought that I was him.

A reporter chap called Brian Staley was surprised, or pretended to be surprised, to find none of his old friends still there. He was interesting and we got on well. He did have a beard like mine and now thirty years later it occurs to me that he might have been the girl's previous friend.

One evening three policemen banged furiously at the gate. I was afraid to let them in or to keep them out. I could think of no reason for them being there. I thought it just possible that they could arrest me and I would disappear. As a foreigner with a proper visa I should be safe but only if the Embassy knew what had happened and there was no way to get in touch with them quickly. My servant's boy friend Dan Ong (about whom more later) was visiting. While I worried, Dan let them in - in some haste! The policemen searched the house quickly, had a word with Dan Ong, and left. There was little of value or interest in the house and it was just as well the machine gun was gone.

One evening Tan said: "*Fini gaz.*" A terse Vietnamese expression which means: "You have run out of propane. Of course, the shops are closed and do you want raw beans for supper?"

Being a man of great resource I hooked some petrol out of the Land Rover and fired up my little petrol stove. Fifteen minutes later there was a knock at my door and a voice calling: "Sirr! Sirr!"

I hurried downstairs and saw the whole stove covered in flames, about to burst and shower burning petrol over the girl who was leaning over it; I was unable to shoo her away to a safe distance! Being a man of great resource, I ran to the Land Rover, seized the fire extinguisher and doused flames and all. 'The man of great resource' had saved the servant but spoiled his supper. The beans were not only undercooked but also seasoned, beyond edibility, with carbon tetrachloride. For those who don't know, carbon tetrachloride was a fire extinguisher fluid and spot remover called Thawpit. It has a horrible smell. It has also been used as a vermifuge (to treat worms) but even in 1970 less poisonous medicines were available. Thank goodness it has been phased out.

At this stage you may be getting a wrong impression about life in Saigon, so perhaps I had better return to the subject of work.

Dr Joan Guy had insisted that I did on-call at night, which meant sleeping in the hospital and cross-matching blood or examining throat swabs for diphtheria. I did this faithfully between her leaving and Dr Douglas Stanley, her replacement pathologist, arriving after a gap of six months or more. The cross matches were done by a simple Majeur and Mineur technique on microscope slides to check there would be no untoward reaction when the patient was transfused with the donated blood. I learned enough Vietnamese

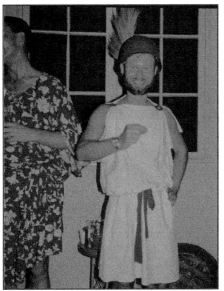

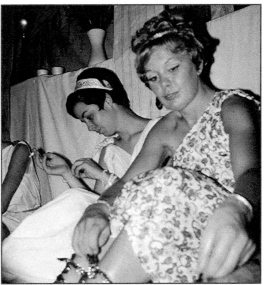

Me! I was wearing this bed sheet when I was stopped at the roadblock.

Alex Clokie and Pam Fisher at the 'Roman Orgy' party.

My paper Roman architecture, designed for the 'Roman Orgy' party with the help of surgeon Dr John Clarke, who also produced the plaster statue of Bacchus, with an enamel mug (drinking vessel) in his hand!

Party staff at Roman Orgy.

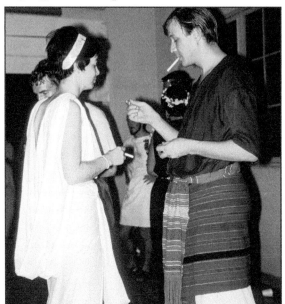

Surgeon John Clarke, my mentor, and Alex Clokie at the 'Roman Orgy'. They were married in Vietnam. Below, Alex pictured with Mr Bohn, the surgeon and Dr Douglas Stanley.

to read the rather simple requests on notes from the wards: 'Please give the results on so-and-so for 1B ward', or on the request cards: 'Please cross-match American blood' or just 'Please cross-match blood'. And I could also write replies like '*Het roi mau my*', which meant that there was no American blood left. Dr Stanley, my new boss, agreed with me that on-call was better done by a local technician who spoke the language.

Dr Stanley brought out with him, from England, two tons of bacteriological supplies, and I was really able to get the bacteriology into full swing. There was known to be cholera in Vietnam. I was unfamiliar with cholera which I had only seen described in books. I got Monsieur Tam to take me to the 'Institute Pasteur' (in Pasteur Street, no less) where they very kindly gave me a culture of Vibrio cholera var. Inaba in a Castenader's bottle.

Cholera only grows on an alkaline medium. We could get American dried bacteriological media, distributed through the *Bo-Y-Te* (Ministry of Health) supply depot at Phú Thọ. Phú Thọ is actually the name of a suburb of Saigon, where the race track is. When we said Phú Thọ we meant the supply depot. I made up an alkaline medium and grew the culture of Vibrio cholera. I kept the petri dish (*Pot de Petri*) with the culture of cholera at the back of the bench and looked at the dish daily to fix the 'naked eye' colonial appearance in my mind. It is generally bad practice to keep plates with pathogens on the bench longer than needed, but remember that Dr Fleming discovered penicillin on one of the petri plates that should have been thrown out.

I was absolutely horrified one morning, on arriving at work, to see a trail of ants coming out of the wall, across the bench, up over the side of the petri dish, under the lid - it was a bit mysterious - into the culture of cholera and back again along the same trail into the wall of the laboratory.

I asked Dr Stanley if we should get everyone in the hospital vaccinated against cholera. I was really worried. Dr Stanley actually had more sense. He said "Keep quiet about it" and I have done until now. There was no epidemic of cholera. I would have known if there had been because I would have found it and it would have been the Inarba variety.

Cholera vaccinations were rather nasty, giving limited protection and only for six months at that. It was beginning to be realised that cholera is not all that dangerous if the sufferer can be kept hydrated. We used to give our vaccination certificates to Mr Luan to get them stamped without actually being re-vaccinated. I wonder if the apparent reduced effectiveness of the BCG vaccine against tuberculosis in recent years, might be due to a similar practice.

I worried that my failure to find things was due to faulty technique. When I did find things I then worried that I should have found more. Mr Bohn, the Team surgeon, said: "There's a lot of TB. I know it from when I was training; there was still TB in England then." I hardly found any, until my servant lady developed a nasty cough. Jeanne Noble, the head nurse, suggested that she might have TB. My servant's sputum was absolutely full of TB. I'd been staining control samples from the Pasteur Institute and could find no fault with my technique, so I could not understand why I found so few cases.

A member of the Team had chronic diarrhoea and I looked in her stools time and time again but never found the Entamoeba histolytica I expected. Her amoebic dysentery was only diagnosed properly when she returned to Cardiff. I found far less typhoid than was thought to be around. There was a theory that anti-malarials could supress amoeba enough to make them difficult to find and the typhoid cases might have been treated before the specimens were sent to the lab. I am not sure about this.

The British Medical Team at Vũng Tàu.
Left to right: Dr Joan Guy, Dr William Collis, Mrs Andrea, Dr Sheilah Beningfield and my counterpart
from the Australian civilian team, Bruce Monday.

Two technicians from the lab, Cô Tình on the right.
One weekend I took a Land Rover load of my laboratory colleagues to Vũng Tàu.

A modest old lady.

Vietnamese at Vũng Tàu which we visited for 'Rest and Recuperation'.
The lady with the yoked baskets is a snack seller.

Montagnard girls carrying a good load of firewood.

CHAPTER 8

FURTHER AFIELD

There were various foreign medical teams in Vietnam. The Australian civilian team at Vũng Tàu (Cap Saint Jacques) were most hospitable, in return for our helping them when they had business in Saigon. This enabled us to take occasional holidays by the seaside, or in country R&Rs (or Rest and Recuperation…)

There was also an Australian military hospital, which I visited twice. The lady pathologist there told me that they thought it politic to diagnose and treat the nearby prostitutes as this would benefit the health of their army and she could not understand why the US army hospitals did not do the same. Vũng Tàu was about 70 miles from Saigon and we had Embassy permission to drive there, if the Military Attaché thought that the security situation was safe at the time.

At Vũng Tàu I met an Austrian doctor in the Australian Army. (Care with the nationalities here!) The doctor had taught himself two thousand words of Vietnamese by using flash cards with Vietnamese on one side and English, (or was it Austrian?) on the other. Vietnamese is a tonal language, and the doctor said he was tone deaf and his patients never understood him. One day he met an English-speaking Vietnamese journalist who told him:"Forget about rising and falling pitch. Just use the following rules for the five tones. For the no-tone tone say the word naturally. For the rising tone say the word short. For the falling tone say the word long. For either of the query tones repeat the vowel sound and for the heavy tone put a 'k' sound after the vowel.

"It was the greatest discovery of my life," the doctor told me. "It worked. The Vietnamese understood me. Overnight I had a working vocabulary of two thousand words."

Yes, you have counted right, there are in fact six tones in Vietnamese but as the mid even tone or no-tone tone was unmarked with a diacritic, it used not to be counted as one of the five tones. Nowadays, Vietnamese is acknowledged to have six tones.

At the time, I was having lessons from Mr Luan. He pooh-poohed the Austrian doctor's pronunciation system but I noticed that he corrected me less when I bore the rules in mind. I learned enough to be able to read aloud more or less understandably to the Vietnamese, but not to me! Mr Mau thought this most odd. The Alexandrian Orthography is the grand name for the system of writing Vietnamese using the Roman alphabet with added diacritical marks. It is primarily phonetic, compared to English. The use of this writing system has no doubt made it easier for the Vietnamese to connect with the West but distanced them from the Chinese. They are a bit ambivalent about the Chinese anyway; Hai Bà Trưng street in Saigon was named after the two Trưng sisters who were heroes in the struggle against China.

Tây Ninh was about sixty miles northwest of Saigon and the centre of the Cao Đài religion. You must understand that Cao Đài-ism is superior to other religions because it incorporates them; a sort of superiority by ingestion. The list of their saints includes (or is it, *did* include?) Winston Churchill and Jesus Christ. Tây Ninh province was thought to be relatively safe as the Cao Dais were anti-Viet Cong. A party of us, part Embassy staff, part Medical Team and one or two friends, drove there one day to visit the great Cao Đài Temple. Jeremy, one of the friends, was able to translate the inscriptions which were about the great amnesty of God.

Lái Thiêu was within driving distance of Saigon and we could go there when allowed by the Defence Attaché. Lái Thiêu produced pottery. Tons of it. As you can see from the photographs it was a rather watery place. The eccentric 'Coconut Monk', was said to be there.

When Dr Guy's replacement, Dr Stanley, was due to arrive, John Clarke said to me: "I've always found my bosses are much more appreciative of my help when they've had to manage without me. I advise you to arrange leave for when Dr Stanley comes, or just after. Why don't you apply to Dr Pat (Patricia) Smith, at Minh Qui Hospital in Kontum, where she works for the Montagnards, and see if you can go there for a working holiday."

Dr Stanley got wind of this and delayed my leave for a week or two but I did get to Minh Qui hospital. I flew by Air America, said to be the CIA's own airline. The flight was free.

I have been asked who the Montagnards are. The word is, of course, French, meaning mountain person. The various tribes in the highlands have taken up the word and now refer to themselves as Montagnards. The Montagnards were the original inhabitants of Vietnam who either lived in the highlands or were pushed there by the invading Vietnamese who spread down the coastal plains from the north. The Montagnard languages are either Mon-Khmer or Malayo-Polynesian and non-tonal. I had thought that Vietnamese was a Chinese dialect but I have since read that originally it was not even in the Sino-Tibetan language group. However it has absorbed much Chinese.

Dr Pat Smith, *Ya Pogang Tih*, was a large American lady. In Bahnar, *Ya* is an honorary title which can be translated as Grandmother. *Pogang* means medicine and *Tih* means big. The hospital was called, in Vietnamese, *Bệnh-Viện Minh Qui* and in Bahnar: *Hnam Pogang Minh Qui* which translates as the Minh Qui house of medicine. I do not remember who Minh and Qui were but the hospital was named after them at the Bishop's request.

Dr Pat Smith showed me the newly-built Minh Qui hospital three klicks (kms) out of town. There was a male ward, a female ward and an administrative block, all single storey and radiating out from the theatre (surgery) in a nice grassy field. One night the unspeakable Viet Cong had raided the hospital and thrown a grenade into the pathology lab, which killed two technicians sleeping there. They had abducted a German nurse called Renata Kuhnen, and kept her captive for over a year. After the raid the hospital relocated to a commandeered school in town. The out-of-town Minh Qui was only used for storage and nobody went there after dark; such a waste of a pleasant spot. I wonder what it is like now and if the .50 calibre bullet hole is still in the store room wall. Renata, who was freed by the Vietnamese Communists and accompanied to Kontum by a group of some 40 Montagnards, was reputed to have sold her story to a German magazine for 20,000$, a sum of money equal to about five times my then annual UK salary.

At Minh Qui I met Geoff Bulley, general factotum and engineer extraordinaire. I helped him transfer the rear half-shafts from a Land Rover with a good front axle to a Land Rover with both axles broken. The little Deux Chevaux, used for commuting here and there, ruptured its petrol tank on a stone when collecting X-rays from Fire Base Caroll. At that time the US army did the X-rays for Minh Qui hospital. By the time of my second visit, the hospital had its own X-ray working. I suggested that after the battery had been taken out, perhaps the car could be rolled onto its side to get at the petrol tank. It was soldered up without the explosion that I feared, in spite of remaining traces of petrol. Only afterwards I remembered that a car has quite a lot of other fluids besides the battery. Not only is there the radiator but also hydraulic fluid for the brakes. However, the Deux Chevaux ran fine afterwards.

One day Geoff and I took the long-wheelbase Land Rover to Pleiku, some thirty miles south of Kontum, to scrounge oxygen for Minh Qui hospital. This was the Land Rover with the broken rear differential. On a road with a firm base, but a smooth cambered surface lubricated with mud, we lost control and skidded into the ditch. This was no reflection on Geoff's driving, the road was so slippery I could hardly walk on it. Geoff pulled out a little notebook from the pocket of his fatigues, looked in it and said: "I think I know someone near here."

He grabbed his gun and walked off. He returned in about an hour with an army breakdown truck driven by two Vietnamese who hauled us out of the ditch. Geoff refused to sign their work chit, as he thought it might get the hospital into trouble. I thought of signing it with my National Service rank and number. If I had it might have created a moment's puzzle to some REMF (Rear Echelon Mother Fucker if you were wondering, referring to a soldier far from the frontline) but it was just possible that it could have started a diplomatic incident. In hindsight, I should, of course, have used the old trick of the illegible signature. Dyslexia has its uses.

I had quite an interesting and exhausting week at Kontum and did a lot of things out of the usual run of laboratory work. Normally I do not mind getting my hands dirty but it is horrible when there is no running water to wash off car grease and mud. It does not help to know that the mud might have hookworm in it.

I visited the New Zealand civilian medical team at Qui Nhơn on the coast of the South China Sea. There my counterpart in the lab was also called Martin. Their team had light NZ Trekka vans. These had NZ fibreglass bodies on a Skoda chassis, the only ones I ever saw. Martin said that he had tried to start a local blood transfusion service but could not get any volunteer donors except for some local bar girls who thought it was an aid to slimming. The New Zealand team ethos was very similar to ours. I visited the *Save the Children* centre there but I never got to the Canadian rehabilitation centre or the NZ military.

New Zealand did have a small military presence in Qui Nhơn and I was given a lift by a New Zealand Air Force plane from Qui Nhơn to Saigon. The plane resembled a World War II Bristol Bombay and had a fixed undercarriage below the wing. I was fascinated to watch the landing wheel rotate slowly in the slipstream. At one point, flying into an air pocket, the plane went into negative G. I watched the navigator's instruments and coffee rise in the air and come down elsewhere. Luckily, we were wearing seat belts and the load was netted down. At Saigon I saw the navigator open the door of the chemical loo at the back of the plane and sniff. Some planes, boats and fairground rides have given me a stomach-churning drop but I have never been actually 'pulled down' before or since. It really was a rather nasty three seconds in my life.

Geoff Bulley, on the left; I'm in the Land Rover.

The Deux Chevaux on its side for repair of the tank.

Tank on the road, Tây Ninh. In my haste to pull off the road to be well clear of the tanks and find my camera I accidentally double exposed this picture of the last tank in the convoy. The tracks vehicle behind the tank is an armoured personnel carrier and not a tank.

Sunbathing on the beach, in the background the ship that had run aground and was never re-floated.
Below: Vũng Tàu was a R & R area for American military and had been a traditional holiday resort for the French. Australians and British used it and even, it is said, the Viet Cong

The Catholic side of the Vũng Tàu peninsula.

The Buddhist side of Vũng Tàu.

The way to Tây Ninh. The whole of the foreground is defoliated.

Buddha at the great Cao Đài temple, Tây Ninh.

Visit to Lái Thiêu, a village of pottery. Colleagues exploring included nurses Eileen Greenhan and Jenny Jones.
Below: Our jeeps parked on the banks of the Song Sai Gon river.

The charm of the river at Lái Thiêu - the Song Sai Gon in Binh Duong province.

The deserted out-of-town Minh Qui hospital, only used for storage after the Viet Kong had thrown a grenade into the pathology lab, killing two technicans and abducting the German nurse Renata Kuhnen.

Minh Qui's water was trucked up from the Dak Toh river and stored in a boat. It was then distributed by bucket, the water being poured into the boat.

At Lái Thiêu - the public loo...

Roman-style Corinthian columns under Chinese arches. Vietnam is on the edge of the Chinese cultural tectonic plate where East meets West.

A watcher at Tây Ninh. I took the photograph to get rid of him...but he did not go.

CHAPTER 9

LEAVE - JAPAN, SINGAPORE AND BEYOND

Besides Mr Luan the other Mr Fixit was Monsieur Pierre at the Embassy. He re-routed my mid-tour leave so as to return to the UK via Singapore, Tokyo and the USA. I stayed in Tokyo at the Akasaka Tokyu Hotel. I was told that Monsieur Pierre at the Embassy never got thanked so I wrote him a thank-you letter in my best copper plate hand. He was so pleased he displayed my letter on his notice board.

I arrived at Haneda airport in Japan and I must have gone through customs and immigration although I don't remember it. I found myself not just a bit dyslexic, as usual, but totally illiterate, as there were almost no signs in English, or the Roman alphabet. While I was trying to gather my wits and orientate myself, a taxi driver approached and offered to drive me into Tokyo. I was a little doubtful but accepted the lift. At the Akasaka Tokyu Hotel I explained that I had no Japanese money, but asked him to come into the hotel while I cashed a Hong Kong and Shanghai Bank traveller's cheque (about which more later). He would not come into the hotel, so I gave him all my Hong Kong dollars, which amounted to about three pounds.

The driver went away somewhat puzzled, but did not attack me or steal my luggage. The trip from the airport to the hotel was about twenty miles, and the cost would normally be around thirty pounds, so this taxi driver came off rather badly.

In the 1970s an almost identical thing happened to my Chinese friend at Heathrow where an unscrupulous taxi driver took almost all his small stock of English money to pay the fare into London. This is evidently one of the things you have to look out for. I now know that airports usually have airport buses or even underground trains into town. Don't go by taxi!

While in Tokyo, Japanese New Year was celebrated, and the hotel staff offered me (free) New Year rice wine. They all kept absolutely straight faces when they served me the sake in a rectangular wooden box. How do you drink from a wooden box? I am more used to cups and glasses. Hoping for the best I turned the box corner-wise and tried to pour the wine into my mouth without touching the box with my lips, which would be rather unhygienic and probably not favoured by the Japanese. They kept their straight faces, but I think they were really laughing behind my back.

I booked a bus tour and went to the hotel foyer sixty seconds late; the bus was already three hundred yards up the road, just going out of sight. Japanese precision for you! The underground and buses were a total mystery. I had asked the hotel staff for an underground map. I looked into an underground station but could see no correspondence between the symbols on the map and the symbols in the station. So I went everywhere on foot. I was a strong walker in those days.

I visited the Yasukuni Shrine, built of the traditional Hinoki wood. This was the shrine for the war dead of Japan. When a son said to his family: "I'm off to war. I will see you at the Yasakuni shrine..." it meant he did not expect to get back alive.

I had practised judo with the Oxford University club and long had an interest in it so I sought out the Kodokan, the world headquarters of judo. This was difficult as I did not speak Japanese and had to ask the way by miming judo. In the end, I did not have the courage to go in.

I explored Tokyo by foot and walked round the Imperial Palace grounds. These are surrounded by a vast moat which keeps the gardens (presumably the Palace is hidden somewhere in the centre), isolated from the modern and noisy suburbs of Tokyo.

I also explored department stores, as I did in New York. Almost the only thing I bought was a Japanese brush-pen. This looks like a fountain pen but when you take the cap off you find not a nib but a little brush for writing Japanese characters. Typewriters and computers of those days could not handle Chinese and Japanese characters, so Japanese business communicated with handwritten photocopied notes. Not surprising then that the Japanese were the people who brought photocopiers into widespread use!

(The great increase in the power and influence of China in recent years is surely founded on development in the mid 1990s of computer software that could handle Chinese characters efficiently. This, together with the introduction of fibre optics and cell phones, has improved their internal communications beyond what even I anticipated. As Napoleon said: China sleeps. When China awakes let the world beware! Well, we are all bewaring now.)

I flew from Japan to Singapore where all I had to do was buy a camera for Mr Mau. The camera shop opposite my hotel briefed me, honestly, I think, about cameras on my first morning there. Later, I was walking along a shopping street minding my own business when a wizard in a white suit turned me into an air-conditioned camera shop. I casually admitted that I wanted to buy a camera. I was shown many different models and when I thought that I had played the naïve shopper long enough I asked if they had an Olympus Trip, the camera that I had decided on before I set out. I was given a chair to sit on and a glass of Coca Cola. I believe the proprietor, out of my hearing, whispered: "Take a taxi to cousin Ahmed and get an Olympus Trip." I was given a second glass of Cola and asked if I would like a suit made. This was all done with great charm and received by me with great politeness. The Olympus Trip arrived. I beat the price down to almost wholesale price, plus taxi fare.

From Singapore I flew to San Francisco via Hawaii and went on to cross the States to New York in stages. Don't worry, you taxpayers, I paid my own way from San Francisco to New York. In San Francisco I visited some distant Oakshott cousins. These relatives were very like the English branch of the family. They were middle-class. They were moderate in their views. They even explained American life so as to make it seem reasonable. They looked like my father's generation, but sounded different, of course. Although of Anglo-American descent, they had never been outside the United States.

I went from San Francisco down to Los Angeles where I contacted David Jameson, an American friend who looked after me for a few days. This friend was part of a civilian road-building team in Vietnam. In Vietnam he'd said: "Well, my father has had a stroke and my mother is struggling, and in a way I'd like to go back to the US to help her. The trouble is, if I went back I would only get drafted into the army and sent back here to Vietnam." At the time I visited him, he had risked a return to the USA.

My travels took me across the States to the Missouri State Hospital, to visit Dr Nguyen, the Vietnamese pathologist who was on a year's scholarship there, supposedly being taught pathology but in fact rather ignored and neglected. I was directed to his room in a large residential block. I knocked on the door, but there was no answer. I knocked again and when he opened the door he said: "I couldn't believe it when someone knocked on my door because nobody ever comes to see me."

On his return to Vietnam after his year in the USA, I took a Team Land Rover to Tan Sơn Nhất airport and transported a very considerable supply of books to his home. Those books convinced me that he really hadn't wasted his time in the United States, although he hadn't learned a lot of pathology. Dr Stanley was firmly of the opinion that he could have taught Dr Nguyen a lot of pathology in Saigon; probably more than he learned in the USA.

I was interested to visit the Missouri State Hospital computer department run by a staff of about thirty. This was in 1970, mind you, and computers were pretty new then. They told me how wonderful theirs was, and that it could do anything. I kept trying to pin them down about the anything it did do: not the anything it could do. Being an MLSO, I was naturally interested in what the computer did for the pathology department. Actually, it didn't do anything for the department itself, except transfer results from the pathology lab to the terminals on the wards. Further questioning revealed that it was mostly used to make sure that the patients paid for every Kleenex tissue they'd used and also for staff payrolls i.e. it was almost entirely concerned with money. They were very proud of the fact that they were working on a programme that could interpret electrocardiograms EKGs, (ECGs in English), sent in on phone lines. Now, I've tried to understand ECGs and have not got very far. It's fairly easy to measure the heart rate, but diagnosing, say, right axis deviation or left ventricular hypertrophy from an ECG was totally beyond me and I was amazed that it could be done by computer in 1970.

After the Missouri State Hospital I went to Mason City, Iowa, to see my cousin Shirley Crosman. Her father, my Uncle Pat Slater, had married a Senator's daughter, my Aunt Theo. Shirley was married to a man in glass, who took me round the nearby double-glazing factory. He also tried to convince me that an electric desk calculator was better than a slide rule. I did not believe him until I started using a calculator years later. Again I found my cousin very like my English relatives. In more recent years, Shirley has 'taken the cloth' and has become an ordained priest.

I had been fixed up with an account in Saigon with the Hong Kong and Shanghai Bank. Before travelling in America they issued me with travellers cheques. I had no trouble with these in Tokyo or in Singapore and changed them without trouble at their branch in San Francisco. In Mason City, I was running low on cash again so I tried to change some more. I don't remember the name of the bank but it was listed in the back of my chequebook. I queued for a long time. When I got to the front of the queue, the teller said: "What are these? We can't change these."

I explained carefully: "These are sterling travellers cheques. Sterling is a kind of English dollar."

She said: "We can't change these."

I said: "Should I write to the Hong Kong and Shanghai Bank

and tell them you no longer do business with them? See here, your bank is listed in the back of this chequebook."

The cashier changed her tune and said: "Well, of course we can change them, but it will take three weeks." I gave up at this point.

When I explained the situation to Shirley and her husband John Crosman, they said they knew the manager of another local bank socially, and offered to try to 'lean on' him. He very reluctantly changed some cheques in this funny money. In New York, there was another branch of the Hong Kong and Shanghai Bank and I was able to change some more travellers' cheques without any trouble.

I think there was a law that banks could not exist across State lines, so US banking at that time was in some ways behind the rest of the world. Perhaps they just did not like pounds; something to do with 1776 and all that? Or maybe they thought anyone, who said 'cheque' instead of 'check', was untrustworthy. Later the manager of the Bank of America's branch in Saigon told me that he could have fixed me up with dollar traveller's cheques, which I could have changed without any trouble anywhere in the world.

I did not realise that there were two Washingtons in the USA and had thrown away my town plan of the DC one. Leaving Mason City for Washington DC, the capital of the USA, I bought a new map and looked at the White House. For exercise I climbed four hundred feet up the stairs of the Washington Monument and found the staircase lined with foundation stones from Masonic lodges from all over the United States. I took the easy way down: the lift.

Making my way from Washington DC to New York, my cousin John Slater, Shirley's brother, showed me the New York Stock Exchange. The greatest concentration of power and money in the world seemed rather dull to me because I did not understand what was going on. At the end of Long Island I met my godmother, Anne Jones Light and her daughter Deborah, at that time married to a 'resting' actor. My godmother asked me what I thought of the actor. I said that I didn't really know any people who didn't work at regular jobs and I couldn't judge them.

She said: "Of course I haven't got a job." So I had to retreat a little and say I didn't know about men without jobs. Of course, I should have said that I hadn't been able to find anything wrong with the actor, but I was still looking, because he didn't make a very good impression. He had fitted a switch on the end of an electric lead to turn off the sound when the TV commercials came on, which he thought very entertaining. Perhaps it was entertaining to an actor, but it did not do much for me. Remote controls for TVs were unknown until a decade or two later, at least in the UK.

The bridge over the moat round the Tokyo Palace grounds. Designed by a Frenchman, I understand.

Entrance to Japan's Yasukuni shrine for the national war dead.

Peter Oakshott, my father's first cousin at his house in Oakland.

Peter Oakshott built this, his house.

David Jameson who took me to Knotts Berry Farm, an equivalent of Disney Land.

Me at Knotts Berry Farm.

Me at Knotts Berry Farm...California's original theme park.

Overleaf *(top): Dr Nguyen at the University of Missouri School of Medicine, Columbia.*
He is next to a Technicon SMA 6 auto-analyser, a 6-channel Sequential Multiple Analyser. SMA 6s were still fairly new then and about as advanced as could be managed before digital computer control came in.
Below: The Crosman's house. This was very unlike an English house. Although on a generous plot there were no fences. From the basement I saw the underside of the living room floor and the odd carpet staple projecting through. Most American houses have basements; I wish ours did. American houses were often on a quarter-acre plot which means that, in town, distances were vast.

91

St Andrew's Church in Singapore, looking as if it was made of icing sugar.

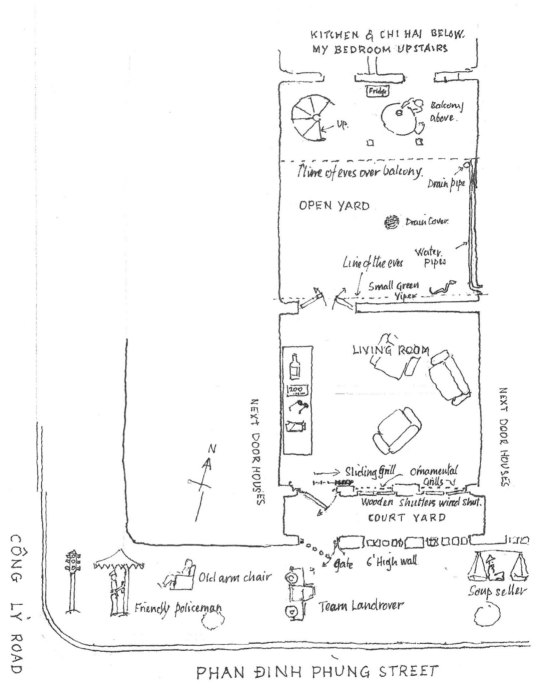

My drawing of the house in Phan Đình Phùng.
I can't remember if there was only one house between mine and Công Lý Road...

CHAPTER 10

LIFE ON PHAN ĐINH PHÙNG STREET

I flew from New York to London and there, for medico-legal reasons, had to contact the Overseas Development Administration (ODA) because of my servant's TB. The ODA's doctor in London asked me if I wanted to be investigated in Oxford or London. I said: "Oxford please" and he got out his medical directory to find a suitable consultant. "No, we won't have him, it doesn't say anything about his war service. But this other chap called Greenhalgh, we will refer you to him."

So I was referred to Dr Greenhalgh, investigated and was thought not to have TB. Of course, while the blood tests were being taken, I knew all the things to say about vampires, Dracula, don't take too much etc.

While on the subject of TB, there is a theory that there is some cross-immunity between TB and another of the Mycobacteria Hansen's bacillus, the cause of leprosy. I was jolly glad of this because in Vietnam I'd visited one or two leprosariums and having a BCG vaccination under one's belt, or perhaps I should say in one's shoulder, was very reassuring. Later, when I visited the LEPRA organisation in Africa they told me that they thought that leprosy disappeared from Europe at the time TB had become widespread, in the late Middle Ages. Dr Hughes-Davies says this is wrong and that he found leprosy and TB co-existing in the Soloman Islands.

Having used up most of my mid-tour leave crossing the United States, calling in at Singapore and Tokyo and being investigated for TB, there wasn't really an awful lot of leave to be spent with the family in Oxford. I did not notice changes taking place. These changes only became apparent to me when I finally returned to the UK. I went back to Vietnam after a week or two in Blighty.

Some of the Team had gone home and everything seemed slightly unfriendly as I did not know where I was to live. The Embassy asked me whether I would consent to live in a little house that had been used by one of the Embassy chancery guards in Phan Đinh Phùng street. As the house was/is typical of Vietnam and comes into the story I will describe it in some detail later.

My servant lady, the one who had had TB, came and visited me at the Children's Hospital. She had been on streptomycin and looked far healthier than I remembered her. I would have liked to have taken her on again, but Mr Bohn, the Team leader at the time, told me: "No! For medico-legal reasons it is absolutely out."

But somebody knew of somebody else who was trying to find a place for a servant. With the help of Mr Luan to interpret, I took this new servant on. Mr Luan gave her instructions to come in to work with me in the Land Rover if she needed anything translating, as she did not speak English. This arrangement worked fairly well.

The Team leaders were doctors or surgeons. One of them was a Mr Bohn, a surgeon from Basingstoke, who quite rightly took it upon himself to tidy up the finances of the Team by cutting some of the Vietnamese staff, painters and cleaners who were employed at the hospital - and who should have been employed by the hospital. Dan Ong (the best plumber in South Vietnam not in the army), was not re-employed by the hospital owing to his trade union activities. He was also said to run a gang of 'cowboys'. Mr Bohn said that he had gone through the accounts and couldn't catch Mr Luan out in anything.

Mr Luan had a sense of humour. When Dr John Clarke married Alex Clokie in a Vietnamese civil ceremony, Mr Luan kept their marriage certificate on his desk. When we asked him why he didn't tell us he said: "Look, here, it has been on the top of my desk for the last six weeks."

The frontage of the house in Phan Đinh Phùng, situated near the junction of Công Lý road, was only about 13 feet, bounded on either side by high walls running from the road to the rear of the plot. One entered by unlocking a metal gate in a decorative wall, took one step, unlocked the wooden front door and then unlocked a metal grill, slid it aside and stepped into the high-ceilinged living room which had its own roof. One exited the living room into a yard. At the back of the yard was a veranda, kitchen and servant's room. There was a spiral staircase up to my bedroom and bathroom, which were over the kitchen.

I imagine this style of house results from a tax on the width of the frontage. The frontages can be as narrow as 12 feet, but the building may go back a hundred feet from the road and up two or three floors. I saw newly-built houses like this on a visit in 1996.

The Vietnamese police (or White Mice), manned the cross roads but did not walk beats. They had a parasol-like rain shelter over the switch that controlled the traffic lights. The policeman at my junction spoke French at least as well as I did. He explained that it had been a rather expensive junction but it was a good investment.

Công Lý and Phan Đinh Phùng were both main roads and a lot of people had to pay him to forget to write their names and addresses in his little book for crossing the lights at red. The policemen controlled the lights and they darn well had to be green for the motorcades of important officials and their armed escorts who drove through the junctions rather fast.

My policeman had made friends with the previous occupant of the house, Jim Marshall from the Embassy, and he expected me to be able to get him a low price drink. I told him that I was not a diplomat and if my consumption of drink suddenly doubled there might be questions asked, though there probably would not have been. I did eventually get him a crate of Singapore Tiger beer, as a sort of insurance against burglary.

The most famous street in Saigon was called Tự Do, or in the Vietnamese pronunciation it sounded more like 'to your'. Formerly known as Rue de Catinat, it was famous for the Hotel Continental which features in Graham Greene's novel *The Quiet American,* and also for the large number of bars. The young ladies in most of the bars were very friendly, but not in one bar which I made the mistake of going into twice. This was either because they were lesbians or because they ran an illegal card school. In one of the friendly bars I rather foolishly gave my address to a girl in the hope of favours to come. No doubt it was a coincidence but I was burgled one night soon after. The so-and-sos climbed the decorative wall and forced the wooden shutter, breaking a metal grille over the window. I think they must have threatened the servant.

The burglars stole two hundred cigarettes, a bottle of whiskey, a small folding slide projector and a pair of sunglasses belonging to Mr Nguyen Van Nam, a square dancer who had left them behind. My servant was such a suspicious lady that, although Mr Nguyen had called at the gate, she had refused to let him have his spectacles even though they were marked with his name in Dymotape. If I had lived in a more generous style, I would have lost more, but as I lived like a monk (well nearly) and had no reason to have a lot of possessions in Vietnam, I escaped quite lightly. Strangely I had had to get up that night to close the bedroom door, which I couldn't have shut properly. The servant raised the alarm in the small hours, and I rang the number that we were supposed to ring. The Vietnamese operator automatically put me through to the American 'Tiger' exchange, who put me back to the Vietnamese operator who summoned a French-speaking colleague who put me through to the police.

In due course a jeep arrived, with three policemen who took fingerprints and confiscated (well, took for tests) the knife for opening the coconuts. When I say knife, it's a thing about the size and weight of a billhook. The police asked me if I thought the servant knew anything more than she had said. I told them that I didn't think that she had been involved. I was afraid they would put pressure on her, or beat her up to try to get more information. I think almost certainly what had happened was that the 'cowboys' had waved the knife under her throat and told her not to raise the alarm until daylight. I helped the policemen push their jeep to get it started.

I hadn't heard anything that night because of the air conditioner which had a three kilowatt electric motor driving a compressor of the refrigerator type. In those days they really did make an awful racket. The cowboys could have had something to do with the girl in the bar, have been casual thieves or even the Vietnamese secret service. I hoped whoever it was would not get at Mr Nguyen when they discovered his name from the spectacles.

As I entered my house in Phan Đinh Phùng Street I used to re-lock the outside gate, re-lock the door and re-lock the metal grille behind me in succession. For about a week every evening the doorbell would ring. By the time I had unlocked the barriers I would find no one at the gate. One day I decided to catch the so and so. I only pretended to re-lock everything. When the doorbell rang as expected I hauled the grille aside, flung open the door and saw a small boy standing on the bottom rung of the outside gate holding on with one hand and ringing the bell with the other. Although the gate was not locked I could not open it without losing him, so I grabbed hold of his leg through the bars of the gate. I wanted to punish him enough to stop him ringing the bell again the next day but not to really injure him. Of course, if I let go he would be off down the road scot-free before I could get through the gate, so I just held on, and on and on.

The local policeman came and said: "*Em khong cowboy...*" Vietnamese for 'the child is not a cowboy'. The neighbours gathered round. It is very frustrating not to be able to say anything reasonable in a situation like this because of the language barrier. Of course, I did let him go in the end and he ran off down the road frightened, but not physically harmed. Later that evening his father, a Philipino who spoke some English, brought the boy round and we made peace and compared notes on what we did not like about the place. The doorbell ringing did not reoccur.

One evening, well after curfew, I came back to my house where the friendly policeman had his lucrative junction. He had an old armchair for sleeping away his night duty, but sitting in the chair was an American soldier. The policeman approached me and asked me to talk to the soldier. I had a word with him and found he was obviously stoned. I thought that in Christian charity I ought to invite him into my house, let him sleep in the living room, and perhaps give him some breakfast in the morning, but I'm afraid I didn't feel very Christian or very well disposed to someone who got themselves into that sort of state, so I quickly skipped into my house and closed the door. I still feel bad about this. In retrospect I see that I missed an opportunity to get another view on the war. In the morning he wasn't there, so presumably, he had been taken away by the American military or Vietnamese civilian police, or perhaps he had just wandered off.

Mr Mau, the chief technician at the hospital, had happened to mention that there was a peculiarly lethal kind of green viper to be found in Saigon and in the countryside. After work, I used to sit in my yard and drink tea while watching the ants carry away joints of cockroach. When I killed a cockroach the ants would come and dismember the carcass and carry the joints up the yard wall and disappear into a crack. The Thanh Lanh gecko lizards left ants and cockroaches alone. The cockroaches were too big and the ants, I suppose, were too fierce.

Anyway, I was sitting there one day drinking my tea when plop, a small green viper appeared in my yard, having fallen in, presumably, from the roof or somewhere. It looked round trying to orientate itself. I called for Chi Hai, my servant lady, and tried to persuade her to get the big bamboo stave I kept for cowboys, burglars and the like. When she saw the snake, she started throwing hysterics, and I had to turn round to her and explain with gestures, as I had no idea what the Vietnamese for big stick is. She went and got the big stick and when I looked round to where the viper had been, I couldn't see it. Out of sight out of mind, perhaps. The servant was less worried, but I was more worried because the parallel walls on either side of the property prevented the snake's escape to either side. The living room and servant's quarters sealed the yard front and back. If the snake could not escape, I thought that sooner or later it would bite either me, or my servant, probably at night when I was coming down for a beer or something out of the fridge. I started thinking and realised that I hadn't really taken my eye off the snake for very long, so it couldn't have moved very far. The yard was bare but it did have some pipes coming through the wall. The hole for the pipes was oversize and it was very near where the snake had been. I went over and had a look. I thought I saw a gleam of something in the hole where the pipes came out.

I had listened to *Children's Hour* as a child, and I knew for a fact that snakes are fairly helpless on smooth tiled surfaces because their scales don't grip very well. They need the grip of the scales to move around. This was all reassuring. I got the pressurised aerosol can of cockroach killer in the left hand and the big stick in the right hand and gave the little gleam in the hole a long hard spray. The snake flowed out of the hole, made a beeline for a drainpipe across the yard. It moved fast and well, probably because it had not listened to *Children's Hour.* I hit at it with the stick.

Now, if you want to kill a snake you actually need a bendy stick because if you have a smooth hard yard and a stiff stick like mine, you've got to hit the snake accurately with the end as you can't get the stick across it, so to speak. Anyway, I managed to kill it and bash its head in. That was the end of that little incident. We bundled the snake up and put it in the rubbish bin. If I had been Chinese or Vietnamese I might have had the servant cook it for supper.

I asked our Vietnamese administrator, Ong Luan, to explain the rules of the road. He very wisely told me: "There is only one rule, just drive so as to avoid accidents." He refused to give any details. Dr Hughes-Davies cured me of accidents in a way more reminiscent of the Zen classics than of orthodox medicine. One day he asked:

"Could you back my Land Rover into the yard, I can't manage it, there are only two inches either side." When I had backed his Land Rover into the yard he exclaimed: "Such skill! Why do you keep having accidents?"

I had to explain to him that the Vietnamese did not conform to any normal traffic rules and were thoroughly unreasonable. In his turn he explained to me that it was their country to be reasonable or unreasonable in, as they wanted. It was up to me to find out how they drove and conform to what they actually did, not what I thought they should do. In other words I had to use my skill to avoid accidents, which I was largely able to do from then on.

Some of the other doctors in the Team were critical of Dr Hughes-Davies; perhaps there was a little *jalousie de metier,* but I am sure none of the other doctors could have cured me of motor accidents. Dr Hughes-Davies treated a lady from the Embassy Commissary for a rash on her hand with gentian violet solution that I made up from laboratory supplies, the only dispensing I have done in my life. I am sure this highly visible stain worked better than a modern anti-fungal, which might have been, in any case, difficult to get there. I am a great admirer of Dr Hughes-Davies.

Soup seller just outside my house in Phan Đình Phùng. The back of my Land Rover is just visible at the extreme right of the picture. Note the image faults on the left and right borders, the result of local processing.

The Land Rover after the accident in the Delta.

CHAPTER 11

SAINTS

One does in life occasionally meet people with some of the qualities of a saint. No less than three came my way during my time in Vietnam. The first was a small pock-marked shaven-headed Buddhist monk who was genuinely concerned about the welfare of orphan babies. He often brought babies with all kinds of medical problems to our Team office at the Saigon Children's Hospital, Bệnh-Viện Nhi-Đồng. He was said to be an ex-seaman and looked like an unlikely person to be caring for babies.

Another was a young American lady, a Buddhist by the name of Lee Eccles, if I remember correctly. She lived in what I suppose would be called an ashram and was well integrated into Vietnamese life. After we heard about an horrific traffic accident in the Delta, Lee, on her Honda, went and investigated the state of the two written-off Land Rovers. She was not a member of our Team and was under no obligation to help.

As it was related to me, some of the Team had driven two Land Rovers down into the Delta on a day's outing. They had with them the Hugh-Davies children and a Dr Nguyet. A two-and-a-half ton truck had collided with both Land Rovers, killing Ross Nixie and badly injuring Jenny Jones, both nurses in the Team. Mrs Hughes-Davies had a broken ankle and Dr Hughes-Davies had glass in his eye.

They were all taken to a US military hospital except for Dr Nguyet who was taken to Cho Ray Vietnamese hospital. In the confusion, Dr Hughes-Davies had mistaken Dr Nguyet for a boy passing by. It was particularly tragic that Ross died as she was a much loved only child and had only recently joined the Team. Dr Nguyet wore her hair short and was small and slim so it was perhaps not surprising that she was mistaken for a boy in the rather confused situation.

Later, though not an especially saintly act, Lee very kindly found a home for four bottles of surplus gin. Dr Guy did not drink as much gin as I had been told to expect. Evidently Buddhists are allowed to drink or at least trade alcohol.

If any of you do go and work in the Third World then beware, motor vehicles are more dangerous than guns and possibly more dangerous than the local diseases. I hear from my nephew who has worked for *Medecins sans Frontieres* that this is still true thirty years later. *MSF* do not let their expatriates drive but employ locals. Of course, the foreigner always gets the blame for any accident. We and the Americans have had large numbers of cars for longer than the Third World and on the whole as regards driving and traffic we do it better. Unfortunately this makes us less able to accept and adapt to local styles of driving. Incidentally, while I was in Cyprus doing my National Service, the only serviceman in my unit to die was killed in a road accident.

The third person with a touch of sainthood was Douglas Gray, a nurse who failed to get a place on the Team, no doubt because of the competition from the four hundred other nurses already on the waiting list. Nevertheless, he made his own way to Vietnam via Thailand and had one or two adventures on the way. He visited several high officials in Vietnam to try to stop the war. He went to work in Phú Mỹ, an old people's home, helping look after Vietnamese pensioners and refugees. There is a picture of the old men of Phú Mỹ in Philip Jones Griffiths' book *Vietnam Inc*.

In Thailand, Douglas Gray was conned out of his money by a drug addict and had to work as a demonstrator of Chinese medicine to earn money for the rest of the journey. Being a 'round eye' he lent authenticity to the travelling Thai sales team; I dare not call them con men. At Phú Mỹ, Douglas Gray cut his foot going to the latrines one night and developed septicaemia. Somebody got in touch with the British Medical Team who brought Douglas to the house I still shared with Dr Collis. Dr Collis gave him antibiotic injections and I made sure that he could get to the toilet unaided and took him his meals. After a week or so he said that he was much better and could I take him back to Phú Mỹ, as his friend there, Harry, the old legionnaire, would take care of him. Douglas wanted to be back in time for the Christmas Eve Midnight Mass. It was easy enough to load him and his suitcase into the Land Rover and drive him there. Later he told me that he had tried to go to the chapel but had collapsed on the way. He had listened to the Midnight Mass lying on the ground outside. He did eventually recover fully and, in due course, returned to England and we all gave a sigh of relief.

Blow me down, Douglas Gray turned up again at Minh Qui hospital in Kontum while I was there. There had been more adventures on the way. The tales of his travels and travails seemed to fascinate the American staff, one story in particular, about buying a slave girl in Thailand. I now understand that the extreme and polite attention that they gave him was due to the difficulty they had with his strong Devon accent. Americans often have more trouble with our British accent than we realise. I have been asked why Douglas bought a slave girl; well it is his story and not mine to tell. But I did say that he had something of the saint about him.

Douglas Gray was a state registered nurse and had cards printed with his name and the letters 'SRN'. He used one of these cards to convince the people at the Vietnamese American Association (VAA or (Hội Việt Mỹ) that he was qualified to teach English. I think there may still be some Vietnamese with strong Devon accents in the Saigon area. The VAA, was where I square danced. Rather like the British Council, it brought American culture to Vietnam; hence the square dancing. I must say that I cannot imagine the British Council organising English country dancing in a country where dancing was illegal!

Douglas Gray, whose right leg is in bandages. He was given a baby to hold at the house of Gordon Barclay, who was the Team surgeon at the time. The Barclays were Quakers and later went on to found the Barclay Centre, which is mentioned in Liz Thomas's book (see p.177).

The green dress is a Vietnamese Áo dài, which translates as long shirt.

Truong Ly Tho in the dark dress was Chinese. She came to my house one evening to ask for help with English. That evening I had been invited out and was already late, as another member of the Team had come round to show me some Thai bronze cutlery. I hastily suggested "Tomorrow?" in Vietnamese. Sadly she never did come back which was a pity as I rather liked what I knew of her.

A Korean lady who danced with real fire, and an American at the Vietnamese American Association (VAA).

CHAPTER 12

DANCING AND OTHER PURSUITS

I had been square dancing in England since 1958. I went to the American Embassy and enquired: "There are Americans here. There must be Square Dancing!" They replied: "Yes!" Go to the Vietnamese American Association or AA (Hội Việt Mỹ) at 55 Mạc Đĩnh Chi Street."

Welcomed as a square dancer I dropped straight into it. The caller was American. The majority of dancers were either Vietnamese or Chinese trying to improve their English. There were also a few 'round eyes', Philipinos and the odd Korean. Except for the Korean they did not, in folk dance terminology, 'give weight', and I found them rather insipid to dance with.

At the Hội Việt Mỹ I made friends with a Vietnamese librarian who spoke good English and asked her about real Vietnamese dancing as opposed to American square dancing. I had in mind folk dancing - there must be such a thing! It was said that dancing was banned because it was bad for the morale of the soldiers facing death away from home while their girlfriends and wives danced the nights away in sinful Saigon. The librarian had a friend who rather doubtfully agreed to take us to see real Vietnamese dancing. The three of us went to a club where the friend gave the password and we were allowed in. Inside they were all doing these incredibly sweaty, illegal and therefore lascivious dances: waltzes, quick steps and foxtrots. I still do not know if there is such a thing as Vietnamese folk dancing.

Colonel Varwell from the Embassy was an enthusiastic Scottish dancer. I attended a few of his frenetic Scottish dance sessions. At one time I was 'care-taking' /accommodated in the Embassy staff residence block in a ground floor flat with a large concrete-floored living room. The solid floor made it ideal for Scottish dancing except the air conditioning was not very efficient. The perspiration really flowed!

Square dancing actually suited the climate much better than the Scottish as it is smoother, and, in any case, took place in an air-conditioned hall at the VAA. Colonel Varwell denied having any special Scottish ancestry but danced with great enthusiasm.

In recent years, on a ski holiday, I met Carol Dixon who said that she had lived in the very same flat when she was working in the Saigon Embassy in about 1972. She had known Pam Fisher from the Team who married Tom Wynn of the Embassy. Where are you now, Pam? I wish you well.

The Vietnamese were rather bad at Western things new in their lives like road traffic and hospitals. They were good at judo and other oriental arts, and being good they were confident and pleasant to deal with. We all went to an *Ecole de Judo*.

I think it happened thus: Jenny Gossage from the Embassy decided that she wanted to take up judo. She was pretty and slim and had nice blue eyes, so all the younger men in the Medical Team, and one or two of the men from the Embassy, decided that they'd take up judo too. I did judo four nights a week, for quite a few months. This tended to rot the judo kit, which had the sweat rinsed out every day by my Chi Hai, but was only partially dry by the next use. The Vietnamese are short and very slim, what I would call gracile. This build with its high surface area to weight ratio ensures they can tolerate the hot humid climate.

I'd never practised judo with people smaller than myself. When we first went to the school they said: "Oh, you've done some before; show us what you can do. Would you like to fight this line of little Vietnamese youngsters?" Every one of them had fun throwing me in a different direction. I only hoped that my humiliation might be taken by them as sportsmanship and it did give me a chance to display good break-fall technique.

After a week, my defensive skills returned, and they had a lot of difficulty with me, simply because I was heavier than they were. I had a lot of difficulty throwing them simply because they were too good. I found myself trying *Kata Garumas,* the sort of throws that people had always tried on me, that is to say the sort of throws that can work on smaller opponents.

The warming up sessions were extremely thorough and scientific. One started by bowing to the portrait of the founder of judo, and then one bowed to the senior instructor. Next we did the warm-up exercises: waggling the ankle joints, flexing the toes and doing the same for the wrists and hands, and finally cracking each joint in each finger. We then recapitulated the process of learning the break-falls. You do this by lying on your back and beating with your arms on the mat, then you throw yourself back from sitting, kneeling and finally standing positions.

After that we would line up and do what they called duck walking, with your bum more or less touching your heels in a very strange gait, akin to Russian dancing. I had never seen it in the UK. Finally in turn we would jump over an instructor into a rolling break-fall on the far side. The instructors were so horrified at my clumsiness that they suggested that perhaps this wasn't an exercise for Europeans. They did not do much groundwork and as this was my *forté,* I was able to make even the black belt instructors work a little.

At the school of martial arts (*Ecole de Judo*), they had very handsome badges on their judo jackets. These badges announced judo, kendo, akido and catch. We asked them what catch meant and they told us it was English catch wrestling. This somewhat astonished us because, as Dr Hughes-Davies explained to them, catch or catch-as-catch-can wrestling is more entertainment than martial art in England. Indeed, the 'catch' word is long lost from our language.

Mrs Hughes-Davies and her son Timon also joined us, not three or four nights a week like me but one night a week. She invited the judo instructors to an English meal. They all came, the three principal black-belt instructors, only one of whom really spoke much English. When they saw the table layout, they made a beeline for the spoons, ignored the knives and forks and ate their meat course with the spoons. The servant lady cleared away the spoons and plates from the first course. This worried Mrs Hughes-Davies who realised that they would have nothing to eat their second course with. I followed the spoons out to the servant's quarters, where I got some surprised and hostile looks. I managed to rinse the spoons for reuse. Mrs Hughes-Davies says that her cook was ready with chopsticks for the instructors but I cannot say that I remember this.

Dave Tunnicliffe from the Embassy was only a yellow belt, but he did weigh fifteen stone. I was interested to see what he could do. He once succeeded in throwing Mr Phu, a black belt who weighed about seven stone. Mr Phu was more or less unable to throw Dave Tunnicliffe. It was only then or perhaps a little bit earlier, it came to be acknowledged that however good a judoka is, he really has to fight in his own weight class. Before that a skilled judoka was supposed to be able to throw anybody, however much bigger.

I had a long weekend in Laos. It came about because Chantal, a French lodger of my mother's in Oxford, had married an Australian law student named Peter Curtis. Peter, who by the way gave me my first driving lessons, went on to become Australian ambassador in Laos, and later Paris. My mother wrote to him and as a result I was invited for a weekend in the capital city, Vientiane. At the morning market there I bought a 'diamond' and two 'black star sapphires' at no great price. I did not really mind when later the diamond was found to be glass and the sapphires, peridotite. It was said that hash (cannabis) was on sale along with other vegetables at the market, but I did not then know what it looked like so I never found it.

Gold was cheap in Laos, well cheaper than elsewhere; something to do with being in the golden triangle of the drug trade. A gold belt for about four hundred pounds would have been good value but in the end I only bought a gold bracelet and three silver belts. The gold belt, good value or not, would have left me short of money and at risk from customs officers and thieves. Perhaps I did well not to buy it.

At the Curtis' house I was invited to make up a fourth at bridge. Although I never pretended to be much of a player I was amazed at how outclassed I was. Chantal's bubbly, cheerful exterior concealed a singularly sharp brain. I don't recollect if we played in English or French. I think all their four children were comfortably bilingual in French and English; certainly the two in Laos were.

Monument des Morts, formerly a private memorial but later considered to be too grand and hurriedly converted into a monument to the national war dead.

That Luang, Vientiane, and a splendid Bottle Brush palm. A 'That' is a temple.

A public building near That Luang. The elaborate roof is quite unlike anything I saw in Vietnam but was similar to roofs in Cambodia. With the open ground floor and high roof it would have been tolerable in a hot sticky climate.

116

His Excellency Peter Curtis, the Australian Ambassador to Laos.

The Australian Ambassador's Residence, Vientiane, Laos.

The road from the Leprasorium at Qui Nho'n.

119

A loom at the Qui Nhơn Leprosarium. Weaving was one of their vocational and rehabilitation activities.

Save the Children's excellent centre in Qui Nhon. The late Dr Joan Guy left her money to Save the Children.

Douglas Gray at the Kontum Leprosarium.

Mido the dog (as tall as a Montagnard) was trying to catch a monkey. The Land Rover was awaiting an engine rebuild but I don't think it was ever revived.

Kontum from the helicopter in which I scrounged a ride.

124

CHAPTER 13

WORKING IN KONTUM - MINH QUI HOSPITAL

One used to meet with Embassy staff at the staff residence's swimming pool. The Defence Attaché, Colonel Coombe, invited me to a dinner he gave for his NCOs and junior staff. My position in the Medical Team was roughly equivalent to that of an NCO. In conversation with the Colonel it emerged that his predecessor at the Embassy had been a Colonel Kirk. I had served in Cyprus under a Major Kirk some ten years previously. We established that he was the same Kirk and quite without thinking I said: "I can't say I ever took to him." The whole room went silent. You did not have to listen for that silence; it sort of crept over you. I realised that all the NCOs had been listening. Colonel Coombe restarted the conversation. As I was leaving after the dinner, a pretty staff sergeant said: "But we always liked Mrs Kirk."

One of Colonel Coombe's staff showed me an AK 47 rifle. It was between a submachine gun and a turn-bolt rifle in size and quite unlike anything I had seen before. The receiver had plenty of spare space for the breechblock and I thought this would make it reliable and dirt resistant. I did not foresee that it was so well designed that it would be a famous world-beater for the next thirty years and more. It was suggested that I fire an AK 47 for evaluation but somehow this never happened and although I would have liked to, I was not in a position to push the matter.

At the pool the Air Attaché's Second in Command happened to say that if I wanted a lift to anywhere in Vietnam they might be able to help, provided the trip could be fitted in with their work. That is how I came to be flown to Kontum for my second visit in what seemed like a private flight piloted by the Air Attaché himself. The Air Attaché and his crew filmed the approach to Kontum airport, landed, gave me a hand with my luggage, had a pee and took off, as they had to be back in Saigon, two hundred miles south, in time for lunch. I asked some Montagnards to keep an eye on my luggage as it was too heavy to carry. It included parts salvaged from the crashed Land Rovers, badly needed by Minh Qui. Setting off on foot to find Minh Qui Hospital, I was soon given a lift the short way to the hospital staff house where Jean Platz, in effect the head nurse, was preparing the Thanksgiving turkey.

When I was there, Minh Qui was in a commandeered school on the low road in Kontum, fairly near the Cathedral. The hospital had been relocated after the Viet Cong had attacked the out-of-town site. The Bishop's palace, or Seminary, and the staff quarters were off the top road about a quarter of a mile up the hill.

Minh Qui Hospital was supported by Bishop Paul Seitz and the Catholic organisation in Kontum. The men on the hospital staff slept in a terrace of bungalow-style rooms in the Seminary grounds, for the sake of propriety. The women lived in a staff house a quarter of a mile away. One night in the room I shared with Geoff Bulley, I woke to a noise and saw a figure clad in tiger-style camouflage at the French window, fumbling for the doorknob. I opened the door and let in Barbara Hutton. Barbara had worked with the British Medical Team in Saigon and had moved to Kontum where she was engaged to Geoff.

Now wide awake, Geoff said: "You silly fool creeping round at night. If I had been awake I might have shot you."

Geoff kept a Karl Gustav submachine gun handy. I thought this odd for a hospital worker even in Kontum.

"Either you stay here till daylight and you will have to share a bed with Martin, or you will have to go back by Land Rover. I'm not having you wandering about in the dark!"

A Vietnamese army sentry box overlooked the grounds of the Seminary. Geoff was pretty grumpy and short as people are when they have just come near to shooting their fiancée. Barbara seemed to be in a strange mood. I think she had taken painkillers after some minor accident. I was not averse to sharing my bed with Barbara as she could not share Geoff's as he slept on a stretcher because of his bad back. However, I thought that the only gentlemanly thing to do was to drive her back to the women's quarters. On the way there, on the grass lawn bordered by the poinsettia bushes, was a great white flare parachute. At the gates to the women's quarters, Barbara said that she had lost her crucifix. So back we went, waking Geoff again. He was even grumpier this time, and we still could not find the crucifix. Back at the gate I had a lucky thought. I told Barbara that a crucifix could always look after itself. That seemed to soothe her and sure enough the crucifix was found the next morning by the gate. On the way back to Geoff's room I gathered up the parachute. These flare parachutes were much valued both as souvenirs and as sun shades. You can see how they were used in the picture on page 38 of the School of Pharmacy. I still have mine.

A Montagnard was brought into Minh Qui hospital and very soon expelled a tape worm. An American nurse, one Barbara Corvino, said that when the worms get out the prognosis is very bad. Dr Pat Smith asked for blood films and suggested that I look for *Pasteurella pestis*, now called *Yersinia pestis*, the cause of plague and thought to have been the cause of the black death of 1665. I found the characteristic bipolar bacillae. I quite cynically went back to the patient and made another dozen blood films as teaching material for my professional friends in England where plague specimens are hard to come by, fortunately for us! Dr Pat Smith told me that she had never saved a plague patient when the bacillae were apparent in the peripheral blood. The patient died.

The Montagnard staff had seen plague sweep through their villages with a very high mortality and were worried about us Western staff. There were thought to be occasional cases of plague in Saigon and I was once asked to try and extract pus from a child's groin swelling which looked, to the Vietnamese doctor, bubo-like (i.e symptomatic of bubonic plague). As a lab technician I would not have been asked to do this in England; it would have been the doctor's job. I could not find any pus and I think there was not any.

On New Year's Eve, the Montagnards held a party for us. There was a circle of low stools (seats if you are American) each with a wine jar in front. Each wine jar had a plastic or bamboo tube going to the bottom. You sucked from each jar in turn and then went back to the one you liked. The alcohol, in the words of Dr Pat, sort of sneaks up on you. As you sucked the wine and the level started to go down, it was topped up with water so the jars were always full but the wine became more diluted as you got drunker. Sometimes the Montagnards put a stick across the top of the jar with a stem dipping into the wine so that they could see how much you were drinking. The wine was brewed from maize, millet or rice.

Rice wine was the nicest and tasted like sake. Sometimes 'special leaves' were included in the brew so it was very easy to get very drunk, as I did to my shame. At the party there was a bronze gong orchestra and lots of noise and jollity, which I have on tape.

I had ear trouble in Saigon until I took Dr Poole's advice and stopped swimming. In Kontum I could not resist taking a dip in the Đắk Tô river and, sure enough, the *otitis externa* returned. My own new bacteriology department was to hand. I found that the bugs causing the trouble were sensitive to Chloramphenicol. The only Chloramphenicol I could find in the hospital was in the form of eye ointment. This surprised me, as it was the then antibiotic of choice for typhoid, of which there was no shortage.

Otitis externa is a closed space infection and because there is not room for the flesh to swell it can hurt. The doctors told me that mine was mild i.e. there was little pus and they were able to get the auroscope into my ear. It did not feel mild. In desperation I made ear drops by diluting the eye ointment with liquid paraffin, which effected a rapid cure.

The hospital held sales of local crafts to supplement their charity money. Ya Vincent sold me two crossbows. Dr Poole, of the Medical Team, got one of them and I still have the other. Geoff Bulley gave me a third, which had split but was repairable. An old Montagnard showed me how to load them and told me: *"Ah, vous comprenez, Monsieur, c'est Le Fusil Montagnard."* The release mechanism is made from a single cunningly-shaped piece of bone and it is very sensitive. The whole thing is said to be made and polished using only a Montagnard knife. They also sold knives and hand-woven cotton blankets and shoulder bags. The knives were of traditional appearance, but actually made from vehicle springs and not tempered to a hard edge. The blankets looked like the traditional ones but being made with colourfast American thread, they were actually better than the native ones.

Minh Qui had a vast amount of beautiful American volumetric glassware. Jean Platz asked me to sort out what was needed and what was surplus. I put aside enough glassware to last the laboratory at least ten years. One of the priests in the Seminary taught chemistry and was happy to take the remaining three quarters of the total. One or two small volumetric flasks went to the nuns as elegant little tulip vases.

I was asked how to make kerosene for the oil lamps from gas oil and gasoline. With so much excellent glassware available it was an easy matter to measure the specific gravities of the gasoline, gas oil and last remaining kerosene. Calculating the ratio and making a mixture with the right specific gravity was routine to an MLSO, but like mixing whisky-sodas with vodka instead of soda, it was bad chemistry and possibly dangerous. I test-fired some of the mixture and it seemed to combine the undesirable and dangerous properties of its parent ingredients. It ignited explosively and then burnt with a sooty flame. I had to warn of its dangers and deny any responsibility for possible accidents. The Bishop's generator was closed down at the end of each day, and with no electric light at night it really was needed. I could not try to ban it altogether.

The staff, New Year 1971. Front row, left to right: Dr Bragg, a Vietnam Volunteer Physician; Noir (pronounced Noa), the dog, myself. Next row: Sister Calixt, Ong Nglau (in jacket with red on it) and others… Back row: a visiting doctor; Mike Coles, the paramedic; Jean Platz and Bok Henning Leibnitz, the German nurse. Bok is a Bhanar title which can be translated as Mr, Ong is the Vietnamese equivalent.

The laboratory in the corner of the main ward.

Right: Dr Bragg at the microscope, an American GP visiting on the Vietnam Volunteer Physician's program. As there was no electricity inn the afternoon, we had to take the microscope outside to catch the light.

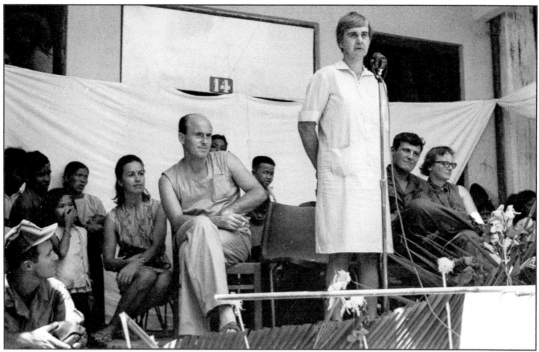

Dr Pat Smith giving a speech. The bald man on the left is 'Bok' Henning Liebnitz a German nurse and right hand man in the hospital. To the right of Pat is a visiting army doctor and to the right of him is Jean Platz who got lumbered with most of the hospital administration.
Below: Dr Pat Smith and her adopted Montagnard son, Det. Pat, not Det, is doing the drinking...

Three Montagnard boys.

Montagnards doing a little dance with a setting step used in dance the world over, including England and Scotland.

Tug of War at the New Year party. Mido the dog is looking on...

Vietnamese on the top road.

Bok Henning and some friends of his from the German hospital ship at Nha Trang on the top road near the Bishop's palace.

The Đắk Tô River which brought on my ear trouble.

The Bishop's palace and Seminary viewed from the top road in Kontum. It was a wooden framed structure rather in the Tudor style. The Men's quarters where I lived (see below) were behind this magnificent frontage.

Above: Vietnamese houses were built on the ground. Montagnard houses are built on stilts like this one is going to be. The animals can live underneath if required.

Ho Chi Minh lived among the Montagnards for a time in his travels and his beautiful house in Hanoi is built on stilts in Montagnard-style.

Steps to a Montagnard house.

137

Me with a rat trap made without metal. The Montagnards ate rats; indeed they ate almost everything. Two of the early French missionaries, Durisbour and Simonet, are reputed to have asked the Montagnards what they ate: "We eat everything that swims, runs, crawls or flies. It would have been easier if you had asked us about the four things that we don't eat." Rat fleas sometimes carry plague. Years later I have been told that Mike Coles, because of this, advised the Montagnards to roast their rats still in the traps. I imagine that they must have been able to get hold of metal traps by then.

Kontum Cathedral on the low road.

The kitchen. The rear pot has bottles of formula (baby food) in it.

139

My blanket (photo below) was woven on a Montagnard loom like this.

140

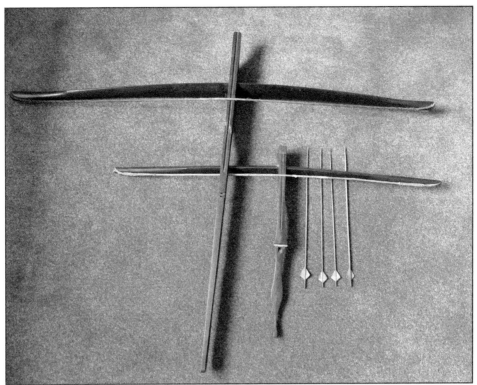

Below, Dr William Collis's crossbow and quiver similar to mine above.

141

One Tom Carlton had been drafted into the US army and had served in Vietnam. After demobilisation he came back as a civilian worker at Minh Qui. I wonder if this was to make amends for the things he felt guilty about. I imagine that they were things he had seen rather than done. He lived on dry bread and tea without milk. Not too much of either I may add. He had no special medical training and seemed to be in a dream all the time.

On New Year's Day, I had to fly from Kontum to Saigon to arrange my visa and flight home. I was asked to keep an eye on Tom and see that he got to CMRI (Catholic Medical Relief International) in Saigon. I was airsick and had a four-plus hangover from the party. Tom was utterly tranquil as he had abstained from strong drink and almost all food for a month or so.

Where we changed planes at Qui Nhon, it was he who said: "I don't think that's the right plane…" and made sure that we both got to Saigon. We were met at Tân Sơn Nhất airport by CMRI, so Tom did get into their care. Two weeks later, the Minh Qui staff rounded on me: "What did you do with Tom Carlton? We have just had a frantic call from his parents in the USA." I had some trouble shifting the blame on to CMRI in Saigon.

Telephone calls through the civilian PTT were very difficult but eventually CMRI were contacted and they confirmed putting Tom on a plane for America. A fortnight later it emerged that Tom had left the plane at San Francisco and set off to hitch-hike the 2,000 miles to his home without saying anything to anyone. Years later I read in the Minh Qui newsletter that Tom Carlton had made the biggest contribution of any single individual to the hospital fund.

Over New Year in Saigon, I bumped into intern Dzi, whom I knew slightly as he had worked at Nhi Dong. He was, by then, a fully qualified doctor. He told me that he had been posted to Phú Quốc island where Viet Cong prisoners were held by the South Vietnamese. Dr Dzi told me that there were 60,000 prisoners on the island and that 40,000 of them were ill. He wanted to make it his life's work to look after them with the help of a pathologist. The pathologist had a microscope but would only go to Phú Quốc if he also had a spectrophotometer.

Dr Dzi had found an old French spectrophotometer for sale. I said that I knew about spectrophotometers and could look over the one that he had found. I advised Dr Dzi against buying it as it came with only one cuvette, a flat-sided little glass or quartz tube, and in an uncommon size at that. Spare cuvettes, let alone spares for the machine itself, would be impossible to find. Cuvettes, good ones at any rate, are expensive and breakable; one does need spares.

In those days, nearly all laboratory work ended up under a microscope or in a spectrophotometer. I remembered that the Nhi Dong laboratory had four rather basic American Coleman spectrophotometers and only used two of them. They produced adequate results with readily available round test tubes. May God forgive me for this, I am sure that Dr Nguyen never did.

I said to Dr Dzi: "Dr Nguyen, the Pathologist, is back from the USA. Why don't you go and negotiate with him the use of one the four spectrophotometers, perhaps on a long loan or some special Vietnamese arrangement."

I soon heard Doctors Dzi and Nguyen in long and loud argument. The last time I was in Saigon, Dr Dzi thanked me for my help and gave me a pipe, a pair of chop sticks and a small carved turtle. He explained that these were carved from the heart wood of the wild tea tree of Phú Quốc island. The heart wood is only a few centimetres wide and is the hardest and rarest wood in the world.

A Medivac helicopter has just taken off. Mike Coles, the paramedic, is on the extreme left.
American helicopters sometimes brought us ill or injured Montagnards or oxygen from Pleiku.

The chopsticks, turtle and pipe made from heartwood given to me by Dr Dzi. The turtle symbolises independence, longevity and intelligence in Vietnamese culture.

144

CHAPTER 14

WHIZZ BANGS

In Kontum things tended to go bump in the night and, occasionally, in the day. The bang-whizzes came from 'outgoing' 155mm artillery shells. The 'bang' was from the gun being fired and the 'whizz' was the sound of the shell in flight. 'In-coming' went whizz-bang. The whizz from the rocket as it flew over and the bang when it exploded. One listened carefully! One day there was a whizz-bang, a not particularly loud one. Not very much later, one of the hospital staff came into the house and announced: "A rocket has hit a house near the airfield and the son of the house got blown in half and they have the top half on the kitchen table."

Several of the American staff and, I am sorry to say, a British nurse from Hong Kong, went off to take photos. I thought it a quite unforgivable thing to do. The Vietnamese family had already suffered more than anyone could be expected to endure without people barging in with cameras. I half hoped the family was already in so much shock that they might not notice the intrusion.

It was explained to me that when a rocket landed on Kontum the Americans backtracked it to Rocket Ridge, which overlooked the town. This took one minute. The Vietnamese army command then required four minutes to confirm that they had no troops in the area. Five minutes after the whizz-bang, we heard a bang-whizz or two as some 155mm shells at $800 a time were fired at where the rocket had come from. These blew some trees to bits. The Viet Cong had long before retired to the far side of the Ridge and no doubt sat there laughing.

One morning, before breakfast, Mike Coles and I heard firing. We stood on the veranda of the Seminary looking towards the noise. Mike Coles was ex-US Army and had returned to Vietnam after training for a year as a paramedic (a sort of American Bare Foot Doctor). He said: "The Viet Cong are attacking the MACV headquarters."

We listened carefully. I remarked that there was no machine gun fire, only individual bangs. Then the sky lit up and I dropped to the ground before a possible blast wave could reach us. There was no blast wave, just a louder bang a second or two later. Blast waves, like thunder, travel at the speed of sound, five seconds per mile. We found out later that some Montagnards had been cold in the early hours of the morning and had lit a fire in the ammunition dump they were guarding. They had escaped before the big bang.

Minh Qui hospital scrounged oxygen from the US Army. At the time of my second visit it came by helicopter from Pleiku, fifty klicks to the south. I told the pilot that I had been nearly two years in Vietnam and never had a ride in a helicopter. He said: "Be my guest." I asked about the officer waiting nearby. The pilot said: "I am the captain of this ship and if I say you can come then the Colonel will have to wait!"

The two crew members sat on loose cushions with their feet dangling over the side keeping a look out for VC activity. The Hueys flew with the doors open. I realised that because a helicopter hangs from its rotor, there can be no side thrust when it corners, hence the loose, though rather heavy, cushions. It just bounces up and down a little like an 1100 horse-power motorbike. The pilot told me that a Huey could fly at 120 knots and burned 600 pounds of fuel an hour just screwing itself into the sky. Apart from the noise, a helicopter flight is just like the childhood dreams of flying we all must have had.

One day I was going to the house in the jeep. Jean Platz said to me: "Could you keep an eye on this package and see that it gets to the house. It is very important!" I placed the small brown paper package in the back of the jeep. Jean again said that it was very important and I again said that it would not fall out of the jeep and yes, I was keeping an eye on it. At the house the package was opened in front of me. I had never seen so much cash! It contained the month's wages for the entire Montagnard staff, equivalent in local currency of my entire UK annual salary!

On one occasion, an American soldier had volunteered to give a pint of blood. Dr Pat Smith asked me if I had ever taken a pint of blood from a donor. I said no, but I had seen it done. She asked me if I thought I could and I said that I would rather do it under supervision. "Well, there is no one spare, you will have to do it by yourself."

I was given a Fenwall pack to take the blood in. This is a plastic bag with an integral tube ending with a big needle. When I had assisted in taking pints of blood, from haemochromatosis patients, our taking sets were made up from a pint-sized glass bottle and various other bits and tubings. However, the Fenwall pack looked simple enough so I went ahead, cleaned the arm (they don't nowadays) and stuck the needle in the large and healthy vein. No blood!

Now at that stage in my career I had done about 3,000 veni-punctures and I knew a good vein when I saw one and his was one of the best. There was no one nearby to call for help (well, to get help from quietly). So there was nothing for it but to try the other arm at the other side of the bed. On the way round the bed I realised that there was a little ball in the tube, close by the pack, that had to be massaged out of the way, it being a sort of internal stopper. Once this was done the blood flowed well, but I left a soldier with a hole in each arm and even more distrust of people with English accents.

Americans tend to distrust us anyway because the mad or bad guys in American films often have English accents. I should have explained why I had had trouble and apologised there and then. Mike Coles explained to me that American soldiers only visited the hospital because there were known to be 'round eye' nurses there. I was the wrong sex yet again.

Years later, when volunteering to give blood in England, this event came to mind so vividly that I broke out in a sweat. The doctor supervising the donor session sent me away un-bled although I told her that the sweating was only fright. Of course, it was not really fright but embarrassment. When I did later give blood it was conducted by an obvious gay just after filling in a form saying that I was not a practising homosexual. He was later taken off blood donation when he caught hepatitis B. This put me off donating blood and I only ever gave two pints. Years later I caught malaria, so now I never will give blood.

Another cringe-making professional mistake happened when Sister Calixt showed me a blood crossmatch to check. I was not sensitive enough to realise that she had doubts about it and as it looked all right I OK'd the cross-match. Sister Calixt was a highly intelligent, but very modest, Montagnard nun. Dr Hoffman, who was deputising for Dr Pat Smith at the time (as she was in America), came back after half an hour and said that he was getting a reaction and was stopping the transfusion.

Sister Calixt found some Coombs reagent but, although I knew what it was, I did not know how to use it. Dr Hoffman told me that the Montagnard boy had a transfusion history as long as your arm. I had completely discounted the idea of anyone in the boon-docks (the rural mountain area) ever having had a previous transfusion let alone several. Transfusions become more and more difficult with each one, due to the build up of antibodies to the minor blood groups. I told Dr Hoffman that I could not offer the more sensitive cross-matches required for any one with a transfusion history. The wasted blood could have been used for somebody else but since it was the only blood we had at the time, the Montagnard boy would in any case, have had to do without. I think, if she had been there, Dr Pat Smith would have alerted me to the transfusion history. The laboratory service at Minh Qui Hospital had been set up by one, Rosemary P Velcheck, and she had done a splendid job. I never met her as she was long gone by the time I arrived. I very much admire her professional skill. I wish her well wherever she is. I would have liked to meet her and compare notes.

In Kontum I got the bacteriology going using the dried media from Phú Thọ. Minh Qui hospital had government recognition and could draw on Phú Thọ supplies, though in practice most of the hospital's money and many of its supplies came from Western charities, particularly Catholic ones.

Beta haemolytic streptococci are identified by the clear rings of haemolysis they make on blood agar plates. I asked Ong Nglau, one of the Montagnard technicians, to take a good syringeful of my blood and we used this for blood agar plates. It worked! We did find the *Beta haemolytic streptococci*. The incubator was an old wooden one. Since its thermostat was broken and anyway there was no electricity at night, I cut a hole in the bottom and stood it on top of the kerosene fridge. The exhaust from the kerosene fridge kept it at about 37C°.

Bottom road near Cathedral.

Sunset over Kontum.

CHAPTER 15

Sister Gloria and my National Service

One morning at Minh Qui, when I arrived at breakfast, Dr Smith told me that Sister Gloria had been shot. I had not been there long and I hardly knew Gloria and even in an earlier version of this essay I mis-remembered her name as Rosemary. I did not have strong feelings about somebody that I did not know but, of course, if one of your colleagues is shot you wonder if you may be the next. One thinks: have I kept out of trouble by the Grace of God or by taking sensible precautions? How long will the Grace of God last and are my precautions really sensible enough?

The story had been that she was taking an American sergeant back to his camp on her Honda, after curfew. A South Vietnamese sentry had shot and killed the sergeant outright and put two bullets through Gloria's neck. She was paralysed from the neck down. Gloria was a 'sister', both as a nun and a nurse. We were relieved when we heard a day or two later that she had died in the US army field hospital.

My view of this incident is coloured by my National Service in our UK army. I knew that some British eighteen-year olds were actually afraid of the dark. A Vietnamese, possibly as young as sixteen, in a shooting war, could well be frightened of the dark, and with real reason! The war was much more of a shooting war than I had realised. As a National Serviceman in Cyprus I wanted to fire my rifle both as a patriotic duty and because I had been taught how. What happens is that you are taught to shoot and then told that you are not to shoot in any circumstances. Well, not quite any circumstances. Actually you can shoot if you follow all the rules about challenging the 'enemy' in the three local languages, three times in each, and then only if they have failed to stop. By this time they are probably out of range and out of sight, so you still don't get to shoot.

In 1956 when I did my National Service, our Army had a peculiar age profile. There were not many soldiers between the eighteen and nineteen-year old National Servicemen and the much older regular officers and NCOs, some of whom had been in the 1939-45 war. We listened to the war veterans carefully. Sergeant M related how he had shot the orderly officer while he was on guard one night. Apparently the officer had approached the guard post and the sergeant had challenged him and the officer had ducked out of sight. After further re-appearances and further challenges the sergeant loaded his rifle silently and "Bang! I got him in the shoulder…" The sergeant never revealed whether he had recognised the officer in the dark and shot him anyway according to the rules, or genuinely thought him to be an enemy. You really should not be out after curfew!

By the time I did my National Service, induction into our army had been going on continuously since the beginning of the war in 1939 and had become routine and on the whole, well organised. Our training was, none the less, pretty basic. Thinking back, we were not cross-trained outside our specialities or even taught basic first aid. In a real war we would either have been defeated or learned rather quickly. I thought at the time that the American draft for service in Vietnam had been set up quickly and perhaps not all that well. I can now see that America had a problem conscripting an army from a more diverse population than ours had been in the 1950s.

From my reading in the intervening years, I now think that the US soldiers in Vietnam were perhaps better trained than my fellow National Service comrades had been, in the technical sense. However, they seemed to be casual and not well disciplined. I don't know what the Vietnamese draft was like but Mr Mau came back after six months officer's training, somewhat shaken and with worms, *Ascaris lumbricoides*, for which he took piperazine (not carbon tetrachloride).

By chance I happened to be on the flight from Kontum to Saigon that had Gloria's body on board. A Catholic Medical Relief International (CMRI) worker told me that they always tried to get the body back to the USA if they could as the relatives could not accept the death and grieve properly if they had not seen the body. It would be interesting to get an Australian view on this. In recent years, the Vietnamese have bulldozed the Australian war cemetery at Long Xuyen.

Years later, by another coincidence, I read a description of Gloria's death, by a US army nurse, in a book of collected reminiscences, *Nam* by Mark Baker. There were no names, of course, but the facts all seem to fit.

A Montagnard digging a new rubbish pit.
All the waste was buried and burned in a pit about 6ft square and 12 ft deep.

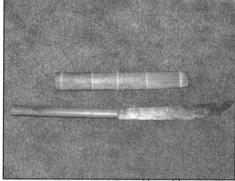

Left: Chopping firewood for cooking with a
Montagnard knife like mine (above).

156

Montagnards making a dug out canoe. The pole has an axe-like blade on the end: spade, adze or chisel, I don't know what to call it. The tool being used at the stern is definitely a kind of adze. I have seen much lighter Vietnamese basket or coracle-like boats woven out of bamboo strips and waterproofed with tar.

157

Dry rice. The short man on the left is Sergeant Stanley, my counterpart from a nearby military hospital.

The taller man on the right is Dr Touy who was working at Minh Qui.

On the same day with Sergeant Stanley and Dr Touy, I also captured this image of a bullock cart in the rice fields.

CHAPTER 16

SOME THOUGHTS ON THE SITUATION

A young Montagnard was brought into Minh Qui hospital. Mike Coles observed: "Those are AK 47 wounds."

Mike Coles and I were in the laboratory corner of the hospital at the time and could not help so we kept out of the way. The story came back to us in dribs and drabs. The Montagnard had been gathering in the rice harvest when the Viet Cong had shot him. What unspeakable swine, I thought.

Another part of the story was translated and filtered back to us in the lab. The Montagnard had his rifle with him at the harvest and claimed to have shot five Viet Cong. My thoughts of fifteen minutes before could not be un-thought but were incompatible with the second half of the story. I was left unable to form a definite opinion on the rightness of the war in spite of actually being there and I still cannot. I leave the definite opinions to the student demonstrators and others who were never in Vietnam.

Bác Sĩ Bach, a Vietnamese doctor, had said to me in Saigon: "Don't be taken in by this Communist anti-war propaganda; we are glad that you and the Americans are here to help us."

There were said to be two million refugees from the North living in South Vietnam and, judging by the few I met, this number could be about right. Dr Nguyen was one of them. They had voted with their feet. I happened to talk to the British consul from North Vietnam when he was on an R & R in Saigon. He gave me a few facts about the diplomatic life in Hanoi but I was unable to get him to say anything good about the North Vietnamese regime. I was left to guess his views by what he had left unsaid. Of course, his opinion, like anyone else's, was coloured by his own experience.

I wondered how much my views of the North were then biased because he had been mistrusted by the North Vietnamese.

In the lab, delay and decay helps with the problem of radioactive waste. The French occupation, or was it colonisation, of Britain in 1066, has had plenty of time to delay and decay. Not so with the French in Vietnam. Perhaps the evils of the Northern regime were induced by fighting first against the French and then against the Americans. The evils of the Southern regime were induced by fighting first against the French and then with the Americans. When the war ended I thought, with the pressures off, the new regime might improve. The Americans remembered their own war of independence against a European occupying power (what British historians refer to as the American Rebellion) and were not altogether sympathetic to the French presence in Vietnam. Of course, the French were more or less out of Vietnam after the battle of Dien Benh Phu in 1954. The Americans were fighting the Communist North.

Dr Nguyen once said: "In a way, I would like the North to take over the South because they would sort out the corruption. The trouble is they would give intellectuals like me a hard time."

Dr Nguyen eventually escaped to America with his family some years after the Communist take-over. He was running a hospital phlebotomy department in California before I lost touch with him. I asked Ong Luan, our administrator, about the political situation and he said that 20 per cent of the South Vietnamese people were pro-government, 30 per cent anti-government and pro-Viet Cong, and 50 per cent just waiting to see what happened. Ong Luan was a singularly intelligent and fair man, so this was probably about right.

I felt at the time that the case for the Americans being in Vietnam was far better than it appeared in the West, though I was still not certain that they were right to be there. Of course, I was out of touch with the slant given to the war by American television of the time. I have read about the war since then and probably know more about it now than I did then and there.

During my last week in Vietnam I got diarrhoea. The diarrhoea was mild but it made me feel more ill than I had expected. Although I never found the amoeba in the member of the Team that I had tested a number of times, there they were, large as life and twice as natural, in my own stool. Just to make sure, I asked Ong Nglau, one of the Montagnards, who said: "Oh, yes, those are *Entamoeba histolytica*." The Flagyl (an antibiotic) I was given did not work as quickly as I had been told to expect and the diarrhoea lasted well into Singapore but not as far as Africa. Flagyl was the then drug of choice for *Trichomonas vaginalis* (an STD) as well as Amoeba.

The LEPRA headquarters and their long-wheelbase Land Rover.

164

CHAPTER 17

RETURN VIA AFRICA

From Kontum I flew to Saigon, where Dr David Poole was all that was left of the British Medical Team. I gave him his crossbow. He took me to the airport for my plane to Singapore and Africa where I wanted to visit friends and delay my return to the UK until the end of the tax year. I was met at the airport in Malawi, by Barbara Hutton, late of the British Medical Team and Geoff Bulley, whom I have already mentioned. They had married and worked for the LEPRA organisation in Malawi.

I am the least observant person but I did notice that Barbara's dress was of strange cut and colour. Barbara explained that in Malawi, under Dr Hastings Kamuzu Banda, women were not allowed to show their knees. The dress was an ordinary one (dresses were relatively short at that time) with fourteen inches of cloth added to the hem.

The Bulleys were very kind to me. I was underweight when I left Kontum due to the amoebic dysentery. Two weeks care and a gentle look round the LEPRA project restored my strength.

I went out on one of the LEPRA rounds. The long-wheelbase Land Rover stopped off at various villages and distributed Dapsone, a sulphonamide, the then drug of choice for leprosy. They showed me how to test the de-pigmented spots on the skin, which can be a symptom of the disease. The patient is asked to shut his or her eyes and a small screw of paper is touched on the pale spot. If the patient can feel a light touch then it is probably not leprosy. Leprosy damages the nerves and desensitises the skin. The patients don't feel and therefore avoid burns and cuts, which is why they get disfigured. As a further test, skin scrapings were taken from the forehead, bridge of the nose and the tops of the ears. A cut about one millimetre deep, too shallow to bleed, is made in the skin. The cut is scraped with the point of a scalpel. The tiny bit of resulting tissue gunge, is smeared on to a slide which is then stained for acid-fast bacillae by a modified Zeil Neilson technique similar to that used for TB. There was a Lepromin skin test similar to the Tuberculin Mantoux or Heaf tests for TB. Apparently 98 per cent of Malawi's population tested positive but only ten per cent showed any overt signs of Leprosy.

At one stage on our round a bicycle was unloaded from the LEPRA Land Rover and an operative was sent off to serve villages inaccessible by motor vehicle. I was told that he would be picked up the next day at the other end of the track by another Land Rover on a different route. If a new case was found, the person was taken into town for hospital assessment.

"Look at this man," an operative said, "we would like to take him in for this ulcer on his leg, but not at harvest time. I will put an oversize bandage on the ulcer and hope that the inner part of the bandage stays clean until we get him into hospital for proper treatment after the harvest is gathered."

From Malawi I went to Kitwe in Zambia and stayed with Barry Mallett and his wife, Flo. Barry had been a colleague in the Southampton bacteriology department before taking a job at the copper mine hospital laboratory. Barry showed me his lab and asked me what had happened to the 'special racing loop' I'd made for spreading the petri plates. I said: "Oh, I've forgotten about it, I don't know, it must have got lost some time ago."

I followed his eyes and there it was on his bench. In Southampton, he and I used to race each other at spreading petri plates both to improve our manual skill and to shift the work. The standard issue loops were too heavy and I made my own out of hollow aluminium tubing. I was also able to phone Sylvia Fearns, late of the Team, who was working by then in Ndola.

Dr Bass was thought to be in Zambia and I did happen to see his brass plate on a gate. As discussed earlier, Dr Bass had left Vietnam so soon after I arrived that I hardly got to know him there. Judging by the stories I had been told about him he was something of a loose cannon and not 'my type'.

Barry Mallett showed me one or two of the sights of the area in his Ford Galaxy. En route, he spotted that he had run over a green mamba, one of the more lethal African snakes! We got out of the car and approached the snake, with far less caution than we should have, and loaded it into the boot. Now I know more about snakes, I know that the biting reflex is so strong that it survives even if there is only a head. A head must be treated as a very short snake. Barry told me that the green colour of the salvaged skin faded to an ordinary brown. If you want to hear a '*When I*' story, as Barry calls them, ask him about the time he killed the green mamba.

A year or two later, back in the Southampton laboratory, Barry showed me colour slides of an African technician doing a strip tease on the media room table at the Kitwe laboratory. He said: "I dare not take these home where my wife Flo will see them and if I keep them here my boss Mr Jacobs will find them."

I said: "Don't worry. Just file them under the lady's name and nobody will ever find them." If any of you work in the Southampton General Hospital Bacteriology Department you might have a look under J for Jesse or N for Nackambula and see if they are still there.

The start of the bicycle run to reach inaccessible villages.

Zomba Plateau near Blantyre, Malawi.

Examining a Plantar ulcer where the callus is very deep and often associated with diabetes.

Barry fishing from the sunken lake. He was well versed in country sports.

Flo. Such a short dress would not have been acceptable in Malawi next door to Zambia!

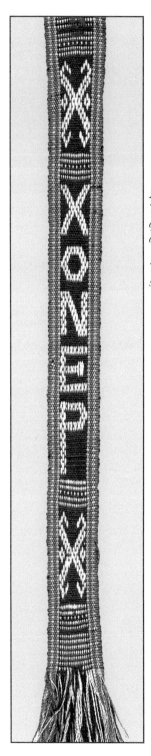

XONEP means Peace in Banhar.
These 10 inch strips were much
quicker to weave than blankets
and loin cloths.

They were given to helpers as
souvenirs.

172

CHAPTER 18

BACK IN THE UK

I flew back to England by East African Airways (run by Alitalia) and arrived after the end of the tax year. East African Airways flew VC10s at the time, which were my favourite plane. These planes gave a smooth comfortable ride, unlike the 707s which were prone to little sideways lurches. Recently, some thirty years later, I'm told the lurches are called Dutch yawing.

Back in the UK I had to cure a rather nasty Dhobi Itch without giving it to friends or relatives, and find a job. Dr Middleton, the Chemical Pathologist in Southampton, had made it clear before I left the UK that there would be no guaranteed job in chemistry waiting for me when I came back and this proved to be the case.

I applied for a senior post in Bacteriology and did not get it. I don't know if they remembered the one or two - well actually more than one or two things - I had done wrong when I was there as a junior, or perhaps they were keeping the job open for Barry Mallett who was expected back from Africa. Barry did get the job. He was a much better bacteriologist than I ever was and also he had a final in Parasitology, so they got the better man.

Bernard Chessum, a friend in London, put me onto a locum job at St James' Hospital, Balham. St James' were happy to take me on. I did not tell them about the ants in the culture of Cholera. I simply said that I had set up a bacteriology department from scratch, which was quite true. They never asked how good it was. From there I returned to Southampton and worked for two years at a University research lab.

I then returned to NHS Chemistry where I was greeted with: "Oh! We have heard about you. You are the chap who used to walk to work carrying a couple of railway sleepers to toughen up.

Is it true that you made a washing machine out of a dustbin?"

Ray Berry's 'Martin myths' had come home to roost. My part of the career ladder had been restructured while I was abroad, and I lost out. However the Vietnam experience did increase my respect for our NHS, which I now thought of in terms of half full rather than half empty. I had seen how much worse things could be.

I had told Mr Mau how wonderful England was. I told him that basic foodstuffs were subsidised. This meant that there was less difference between rich and poor than there was in supposedly socialist countries. I told him that we had almost no inflation. I told him that we had little corruption and we obeyed the traffic laws. I had no intention of deceiving him but when I got back I found that almost everything I had said was untrue.

Decimalisation had triggered off inflation. Subsidies on milk and bread had gone. The introduction of VAT was about to start a tax which falls harder on the poor than on the rich. We had double yellow lines, short skirts and hot pants. Some of the men can't have had a hair cut in the two years I had been away. The one good thing was the start of the Open University. England was much changed and I had not noticed even the start of these changes during my mid-tour leave in 1970.

Dr Joan Guy died in January 2010, aged 89. She had left everything to the charity *Save the Children*, as she had quarrelled with her only close relative. Her executor did not know what to do with a small box of her letters, which were of no interest to *Save the Children*. By a roundabout route this box came into my possession in February 2013, together with one or two documents. At the lab, Dr Guy had always been outspoken and, while never malicious, she was often generous with her disapproval. The letters, at least the ones that came to me, were nearly all from Dr Guy in Saigon to her mother in Lymington. One of the early letters suggested that Mrs Guy keep the letters to save Joan the trouble of keeping a diary. The letters, about thirty of them, are written in a fluent style and a legible, loose cursive script. These are the letters of an intelligent woman of 48. It is a privilege to be able to read them and get a glimpse into her mind.

I started reading with enormous interest. There was not all that much about the lab, but lots about drinks, dresses, diplomats and cocktail parties, things that a mother might be interested in. Dr Guy was determined to make as many useful contacts both in the medical and social field as she could. Americans were a puzzle to her and were often denigrated. Australian men (not Australian women) were approved of. She found the Vietnamese infuriating. (Didn't we all?)

I enjoyed reading about the Team leader and his wife, both disapproved of, and also the obnoxious big-headed young anaesthetist. I thought that it was all splendid stuff until I got to: "Martin is much more dim than I thought. He needs constant 'nannying' which is wasting my time."

I rather wonder if her judgement really was all that good. However in the archive there is a letter from Dr Vu Van Dzi, and another from one of the technicians, thanking her for having taught them so much. I can't read the signature on the technician's letter but she mentions my having taught her to swim, so it must be from Cô Trân Sao Tĩnh who later escaped from Vietnam with her children and and those of her brother and ended up in California.

176

Dust of Life. Children of the Saigon Streets.
Liz Thomas.
First published by Hamish and Hamilton Ltd. 1977. ISBN 9780241894897
(Fount edition: ISBN 9780006250784)

I read the Fount 1978 paperback edition printed by William Collins, Sons & Co.
Liz had lived far closer to the Vietnamese poor people than I ever did. She
got to know them better than I ever did. I would not have had the courage
and charity to live such an insecure life, and endure the consequent health
problems, thefts and setbacks. Liz went to Vietnam on 16th September 1972
and did not return to the UK until 1975 which was after the fall of Saigon to
the NVA. She experienced the first year of the Communist regime and had
a hard time of it. She saw and heard what the people round her thought of
the Communists.

At the time I left Vietnam, early in 1971, the Americans were already starting
to reduce their military commitment. I heard of helicopter 'blade hours' being
reduced. The British Medical Team was also being wound down.

Once a Warrior King. Memories of an Officer in Vietnam.
David Donovan.
First published in Great Britain by Weidenfeld and Nicholson 1986.
ISBN 0297788892 (My copy - Corgi. ISBN 0552 13273 X).

David Donovan's four man team had to lead the local militia against the
Viet Cong in the Mekong Delta. His experiences in the Mekong Delta were
different from mine in Saigon. None the less I recommend the book. I wish
I could write as well and honestly as he did. He gives a masterly description
of some three seconds, when he nearly shot his sergeant and his difficulty in
not pulling the trigger.

Psychological research in the 1980s, by Benjamin Libet at the University
of California in San Francisco, found that the readiness potential in the brain
occurs before the conscious mind thinks that it has decided to act. I know how
good the description is because very occasionally when driving, I find myself
unable to stop from doing a risky manoeuvre that I thought that I had not
quite decided to do.

David Donovan did get to know the local people and speak their language but still did not always quite understand their sexual mores; me neither. He also describes fellow Americans behaving wrongly and how he could not do anything about it. I felt the same during my National Service in Cyprus. I wonder if many people in big organisations feel the same from time to time: I am thinking of people who have to make the best of working with colleagues they would not have chosen. I have never read a better description of the complex and unsettling emotions involved in this kind of situation.

David Donovan also describes how reports were 'optimised' on the way up the chain of command so that by the time they reached the top they had little relation to the facts on the ground. While in Kontum, I read *Our Vietnam Nightmare* by Marguerite Higgins. She also thought that things went wrong for the Americans in Vietnam, because the wrong information was acted on and the right information was lost or disregarded.

On 16th September 2012, quite by chance, I heard David Donovan talk on a BBC Radio 4 programme called Broadcasting House. He was introduced as a retired academic. He said that the lessons learned in Vietnam about fighting insurgency have been forgotten. He said that good results could never come where there was a corrupt government, a hostile population, and where America did not have very sound reasons to get involved in the first place. He was therefore pretty gloomy about the likely outcomes of the present conflicts in Afghanistan and Iraq. I have long been thinking of trying to contact David Donovan and tell him how highly I thought of his book, so it was quite a surprise to hear him and find out that he is still alive and using the same name.

Vietnam Inc.
Philip Jones Griffiths. Collier Books 1971.
ISBN 0714846031 Library of Congress Catalog Number: 73-167932

Mr Jones Griffiths was a Magnum photographer who fiercely criticised the American involvement in Vietnam. The many photographs in the book reinforce the message of the text. His obituary in *The Guardian* newspaper (Monday, 24th March, 2008) states that the book had a great influence in America. Noam Chomsky commented that: "If anybody in Washington had read that book, we wouldn't have had these wars in Iraq or Afghanistan."

I don't quite agree with everything in the book, particularly the bit about the language barrier. Where there was mutual respect there could be good communication and understanding. Mr Jones Griffiths did not mention that the Vietnamese put: "Khong" at the end of a question sentence. Khong means No, or Is it not? Thus the answer yes, means Yes, it is not! I did not understand this when I was in Vietnam: no wonder I was often confused.

Caduceus in Vietnam. A Medical Mission to South Vietnam.
Barbara Evans. Hutchinson: first edition 1968.
ISBN 978 0090884605.

Barbara Evans was the wife of Dr Philip Evans, the first leader of the British Medical Team in Saigon. Barbara Evans observed, recalled and wrote so much better than I have. She wrote at the right time when it all was fresh in her mind. I found, in this book, a fascinating description of the Vietnam of before I arrived, the start of the British Medical Team, and also of Dr Pat Smith and Minh Qui Hospital in Kontum.

Men of Dignity. The Montagnards of South Vietnam.
Paul L. Seitz, Bishop of Kontum.
Edition: Hnam In Kuenot, Kontum, Vietnam.
Responsible for the English edition: J Jackson

This is a book of photographs with a short and respectful text explaining who the Montagnards are and some of their myths and legends.

Nam. The Vietnam War in the Words of the Men and Women who Fought There.
Mark Baker.
Abacus: ISBN 978-0349102399 (Reprinted 1 Jan. 1982

In this book are stories gleaned from interviews with Vietnam veterans. I found them to be honest and revealing. One of the stories is about the death of Gloria. Gloria is not named, of course, but the facts all seem to fit. The stories revealed why America eventually and deservedly lost the war. They also describe the great difficulties many veterans had in adjusting to civilian life. The author wrote: "Until we deal more honestly and thoroughly with the Vietnam war and the veterans of that war, we can't expect to make much progress as individuals or as a nation.

The Sorrow of War. Bao Ninh. First published Hanoi, 1991.
My copy: Mincrva, 1994. ISBN 9780436310423
English version by Frank Palermos from the original translation by Phan Than Hao.
ISBN: 0 7493 9711 X.

I include this book in my bibliography mainly because it was so famous. I found it confusing as to where and when the scenes were set. I wonder if the translators have done justice to the original. The book reminds us that both sides always suffer in a war.

Always the Children. A Nurse's Story of Home and War.
Anne Watts. Simon and Schuster, 2010.
My copy: 2011 ISBN 9781847397898

An autobiography covering from childhood in Wales to working in Vietnam. The sections on working with *Save the Children* at Qui Nhon and at Dr Pat Smith's hospital in Kontum were of particular interest to me as I worked at Minh Qui at almost the time she was there. I had often wondered what became of Dr Pat Smith and her two adopted Montagnard sons, Det and Weir. Age has caught up with Dr Smith. Both her sons are in America. In later years, Anne visited Vietnam but was not allowed to go to Kontum. Therefore she does not know the fate of the Montagnards that she knew there. I also would like to know what happened to Ya Vincent, Sister Calixt and Ong Nglau in particular. Anne has written a second book called *Nurse Abroad*. It is about working with, or is it for, other ethnic minorities in other out of the way parts of the world? It was Anne Watts who put me right about Gloria's name.

My Road from Saigon
Brian Staley. Conrad Press
ISBN 9781911546788

I did not know Brian Staley well in Saigon but I had met him when he called in at the house in Công Lý where he had known Dr John Bass. I met him again in 2016 when he came to a reunion of the Saigon British Medical Team where he told me that he was writing a book about his time in Vietnam and also two later periods in his life. This book was finally published early in 2020 under the title *My Road from Saigon*. He told me that the title had been chosen by his publisher Conrad Ross and that it was not his original choice.

Brian went to Vietnam as a young reporter and came to be trusted, as a neutral by both sides in that terrible conflict and went on to negotiate in the Paris conference that nearly secured peace between North and South Vietnam. In his book he describes the places and people he met and worked with including many members of the team or expat community whom I had known especially Dr Adrian Pointer who was fluent in Vietnamese. On reading the book I found that Douglas Gray, who founded an orphanage, was even more saintly than I have portrayed him. The second part of the book deals with Liberal party shenanigans at the time of the Jeremy Thorpe scandal which he witnessed. In the third part of the book he describes his work in founding the Gurkha Foundation. Brian died in March 2020.

Some Notes on the Photographs

My first boss, the pathologist Dr Duthie, had always encouraged his technicians to make use of the laboratory dark room as this meant that there was always someone about who could take a photograph for him. Hence, I had some knowledge of photographic technique before I went to Vietnam.

I felt that going to Vietnam was going to be the big adventure in my life and therefore I went prepared to take a lot of photographs. I took a developing tank, my old coupled range-finder 35 mm camera and also a Mamiyaflex, a twin lens reflex camera which took 2¼ inch, 6 x 6cm, negatives. The unique feature of this camera was that its paired lenses were interchangeable. I intended to, and did eventually, buy additional lenses for this camera on visits to Hong Kong. I measured exposures with a Weston Master IV meter and later with a more modern Japanese equivalent. I later replaced my coupled rangefinder 35mm camera with an Asahi Pentax SL 35mm single lens reflex which had a 1.4 lens of useful speed but not especially fine definition. This camera was still working well in 2018. The shop where I bought it, Pillar Jimmy in Kowloon, had offered me the new Asahi Pentax Spotmatic with a built-in exposure meter which I declined as I had just bought a new exposure meter.

I developed my negatives in Saigon, but I did not have the facilities to print them. I did get a local shop to print a few but for the most part I had to wait until I got back to Southampton to print them and see what they looked like.

I used Ilford Panf or Kodak Panatomic X, both slow fine grain black and white films which I developed in Promicrol until I ran out, and then in Kodak D76. Colour slide film had processing and UK postage included in the price. My colour slides were all waiting for me when I got home.

Martin Slater is a retired medical laboratory technician. He was educated in Oxford at the Dragon School and then at Magdalen College School. Martin attended the Oxford School of Architecture and failed to pass the intermediate examination of the RIBA. He then did his national service in the Royal Artillery serving in Cyprus at the time of the Suez crisis and later in Germany.

In 1958 Martin went to work in the Southampton Hospital's pathology service. He studied at evening classes and became a Fellow of the Institute of Medical Laboratory Sciences, FIMLS (formerly Technology FIMLT), in 1967.

In October 1968 he went to Vietnam and worked as a laboratory technician with the British Medical team at the Saigon Children's hospital.

Martin paints water colours and square dances.